Slim
Smoothies

Slim Smoothies

Over 130
*Healthy and Energizing Recipes
Without All the Calories*

Donna Pliner Rodnitzky

PRIMA PUBLISHING

Published by Prima Publishing, Roseville, California. Member of the Crown Publishing Group, a division of Random House, Inc., New York.

PRIMA PUBLISHING and colophon are trademarks of Random House, Inc., registered with the United States Patent and Trademark Office.

A per serving nutritional breakdown is provided for each recipe. If a range is given for an ingredient amount, the breakdown is based on the smaller number. If a range is given for servings, the breakdown is based on the larger number. If a choice of ingredients is given in an ingredient listing, the breakdown is calculated using the first choice. Nutritional content may vary depending on the specific brands or types of ingredients used. "Optional" ingredients or those for which no specific amount is stated are not included in the breakdown. Nutritional figures are rounded to the nearest whole number.

All products and organizations mentioned in this book are trademarks of their respective companies.

Library of Congress Cataloging-in-Publication Data
Rodnitzky, Donna.
    Slim smoothies : over 130 healthy and energizing recipes without all the calories / Donna Pliner Rodnitzky
       p.   cm.
    Includes index.
    ISBN 0-7615-2059-7
    1. Blenders (Cookery). 2. Smoothies (Beverages)
3. Low-calorie diet—Recipes. I. Title.
TX840.B5 R627   2002
641.8'75—dc21   2002035452

03 04 05 06 07 HH 10 9 8 7 6 5 4 3 2 1
Printed in the United States of America

First Edition

Visit us online at www.primapublishing.com

To my husband, Bob, who has been a constant source of support in my career as a cookbook writer. I am grateful for your enthusiastic encouragement in all my endeavors, and for being my strongest, yet kindest, critic.
To my children, David, Adam, and Laura, I continue to admire you for your commitment to achievement and excellence.

Contents

Acknowledgments

I would like to thank Prima Publishing, beginning with Denise Sternad, my acquisitions editor, for placing her trust in me to write another smoothie cookbook. Likewise, I am grateful to my project editor, Michelle McCormack, with whom it has been a pleasure to collaborate over these past years. I can always rely on her to attend to every detail and provide invaluable suggestions. Thanks to Monica Thomas, cover designer, and the entire staff at Prima Publishing for their excellent professionalism in bringing this book to publication.

Introduction

Many of us would agree that one of the most difficult aspects of staying on a diet is the daily challenge of finding diet-friendly foods that are quick and easy to prepare, yet satisfying and rich in taste. On top of that, dieters must cope with the incessant hunger pangs that gnaw at them throughout the day or late into the evening as a result of their calorie-restricted or lowfat meals. It can be a monumental task to find a snack that will fill you up but not fill you out. While there are plenty of delicious and easy-to-prepare refreshments that can instantly satisfy your cravings, too many of them are made of unhealthy ingredients that provide few beneficial nutrients and wreak havoc on your waistline with unnecessary calories and fat.

If you haven't already had the good fortune of being introduced to slim smoothies, you may find it hard to believe that, even when counting calories, you can actually indulge in these delicious snacks any time of the day or evening without losing ground in the battle of the bulge. Prepared properly, these frothy glassfuls not only contain a healthy combination of low-calorie ingredients, they also satisfy your sweet tooth. What's more, even though the most elementary smoothies are made with a simple combination of fruit and fruit juice, today's ready availability of a great variety of seasonal fruits and juices give even more rewarding flavor to these wonders-in-a-glass. Beyond the basics, a dairy product such as lowfat or nonfat milk or yogurt can be substituted for juice or included as an additional ingredient. Best of all, you can blend these ingredients in an infinite number of delectable combinations, limited only by your imagination. Health-conscious individuals who are seeking novel and nutritious ways to enrich their diets without adding too many calories or unnecessary fat, will find a low-calorie smoothie the perfect complement to their daily meal plan.

Whether you choose to drink a smoothie because it is a low-cal alternative to diet-busting beverages, for its nutritional qualities, or simply because it is delicious, you can't help benefiting from its inherently healthful ingredients. Smoothies are chock-full of vitamins from fruit, and their dairy ingredients are a rich source of calcium. What's more, you can also supplement these delightful drinks with a wide variety of healthful additives or soybean products that quickly transform them into an even more nutritionally balanced and wholesome treat.

Slim Smoothies begins with a chapter titled "Health Benefits of Low-Calorie Smoothies." Here, you will learn why smoothies are so good for you and find suggestions on how to maximize their nutritional value. In chapter 2, "The Lowdown on the Ingredients: How to Select, Prepare, and Store Fresh Fruit," you will discover the secrets of selecting and preparing the best fruit for the ultimate low-cal smoothie as well as determining how much of each fruit you need to prepare a single-serving smoothie. Finally, if you are not familiar with the equipment needed to make a smoothie, chapter 3, "Let's Get Started: Equipment and Techniques for Making a Slim Smoothie," will tell you what you need to know to transform your kitchen into a Smoothie Empire. You will also discover a host of helpful techniques that let you elevate your blender creations to the pinnacle of smoothiedom.

As you browse through the chapters containing smoothie recipes, you will find that each one is divided into two categories: super low-cal smoothies and low-cal smoothies. I did this to help you choose the recipes that best fit your diet plan, depending on how calorie-restricted it is or may become.

Another feature to look for is the shopping list found at the beginning of each smoothie-recipe section. Each ingredient listed is a component of one or more of the smoothies included, so you can find your favorite smoothies and plan ahead by stocking your freezer, refrigerator, and pantry with your choice of these essential items. Or take a trip to the store and buy what's on the list, knowing you can make any recipe in that section. Then you'll be ready to make your favorite smoothie any time of the day.

Chapter 4, "Sleek and Simple Smoothies," will appeal to all smoothie enthusiasts. You'll learn that all you need to do to make a basic smoothie is combine your favorite richly flavored fruit and fruit juice in a blender and rev it up. Your reward will be a scrumptious, low-cal, and completely satisfying smoothie. Some of my favorites are Melon Rouge (page 50)—a pleasantly sweet blend of orange juice, cantaloupe, and banana—and Cherry Potter (page 42), made with a tempting combination of cherries, pineapple, and banana.

Chapter 5, "Smoothie Digni-Dairies," contains a host of delectable smoothie recipes made with dairy products such as milk and yogurt. You will be pleased to find that adding dairy ingredients endows smoothies with a creamier consistency and richer flavor. In most of the recipes, I suggest using lowfat and nonfat dairy products to keep the fat content to a minimum. However, depending on your dietary needs, you can substitute whole dairy products for low- or nonfat ones, and vice versa. Such substitutions will not noticeably change the taste or consistency of the smoothie—just the fat content, of course. If you adore the taste of cherries, sample a glassful of Bing in 'Da Noise (page 89), made with a luscious blend of guava juice, cherries, banana, and nonfat cherry frozen yogurt. To make an impression on your friends and family, serve Meet the Pear-ents (page 119), a dairy treat made with pear nectar, pears, banana, and nonfat vanilla frozen yogurt.

Chapter 6, "Fortified Smoothies," contains a bounty of recipes made with soybean products, as well as several that feature the addition of other health-enhancing supplements. Although smoothies usually provide a healthy dose of vitamins and calcium derived from their fruit and dairy ingredients, they do not always qualify as a nutritionally complete meal replacement. If you would like to transform a smoothie into an instant meal, this chapter will guide you in the use of nutritional additives and protein supplements to achieve this goal. You will also learn how to enhance the health benefits of smoothies by adding supplements, such as herbs or vitamins. If you are looking for a delicious way to add more flax to your diet, start the morning with a glass of Just the Flax, Ma'am (page 147), made with peach, cantaloupe, banana, tofu, and flaxseed oil. On the other hand, if you're in need of a quick energy boost, consider mixing up a batch of Johnny Bee Goode (page 176), a bee pollen–enriched blend made with soy milk, peach juice, blueberries, peaches, banana, strawberry soy yogurt, bee pollen, ginseng, and gingko.

The last chapter, "Slim Smoothie Garnishes," contains several recipes for garnishes that let you transform any of your favorite smoothies into a visually striking presentation. While some of these adornments are more elaborate, I have also included others that are quick and easy to prepare and can be made ahead of time. You might consider inserting an Apple Chip (page 195) upright in a smoothie or placing a Star Fruit Slice (page 210) on the rim of the glass—each will add a simple touch of tasteful (and delicious!) decoration to the most basic smoothie. On the other hand, you can magically transform a simple smoothie into a light dessert by garnishing it with a Pineapple Bow (page 207) or Kumquat Lily (page 202).

Once considered only a simple combination of fruit and fruit juice, today's smoothies have definitely made it to the big-time. These low-calorie taste sensations in a glass are rich, delicious, and satisfying. And just as important, boredom is not part of the *Slim Smoothies* equation. There are an endless number of ways to blend fruit, fruit juice, and dairy products in a dazzling array of appealing and sometimes exotic combinations. If ease of preparation, luscious flavors, and impressively low-calorie counts suit your fancy, *Slim Smoothies* is just what you've been looking for.

CHAPTER 1

Health Benefits of Low-Calorie Smoothies

With so many people trying to lose weight and develop healthier lifestyles, it comes as no surprise that smoothies have become so popular. Whether these delectable concoctions are made with a simple combination of fruit and fruit juice, mixed with a creamy nonfat or lowfat dairy product, or supplemented with a variety of health-enhancing boosters, the end result is always a nutritionally enriched drink with major health benefits. And with a little more effort, you can add a low-calorie count to these already-impressive health-promoting credentials.

Fresh fruit is the key to making a perfect smoothie. Fruit not only endows a smoothie with a bold, satisfying flavor, it also has significant health-promoting qualities. For many years, health authorities have encouraged us to enrich our diets by including two to three servings of fruit each day. Even with a hectic lifestyle, you can easily achieve this lofty goal by including a smoothie or two in your daily diet. The health benefits of this simple addition can be substantial. Because fruits contain a bounty of antioxidants, eating them reduces the risk of a wide variety of serious ailments, such as cancer, arthritis, and heart disease. What's more, these nutrient-packed powerhouses are also a rich source of fiber and minerals.

While fruits make up most of a smoothie, there are a wide variety of other ingredients you can add to gain an extra healthful boost. You can add lowfat and nonfat dairy products such as milk and yogurt for additional calcium and protein. If you want to incorporate more protein into your diet, adding soy milk, soy yogurt, or tofu to a smoothie gives you the benefits of these products' health-enhancing properties while you enjoy their unique flavors. Soybean products are rich in calcium, iron, zinc, and fiber, as well as being a cholesterol-free, lowfat, low-sodium, and low-calorie food. The addition of herbs and extracts is still another way to heighten a smoothie's health-enhancing potential. Finally, simply by including nutritional additives such as breakfast powders or protein supplements, you quickly elevate a smoothie to whole-meal status.

Smoothies, one of the most naturally healthful menu items, can be made still more beneficial with a touch or a teaspoon of the right additive. By choosing recipes from *Slim Smoothies*, all of this is possible—without exceeding the calorie limit of your diet. The descriptions that follow will help you better understand and effectively use these health-enhancing ingredients and wellness-promoting boosters.

- **Soy Milk and Soy Yogurt**
  Soy milk is a rich, naturally sweet beverage made from soybeans that have been finely ground and strained. Soy yogurt is made from soy milk. These products are high in protein, B-vitamins, and iron. They also are low in saturated fat and packed with fiber. A diet that is low in saturated fats and rich in soy foods is believed to lower LDL ("bad") cholesterol levels. Soy milk is packaged in aseptic, non-refrigerated containers or in ordinary quart- and gallon-size milk containers found in the dairy case of most supermarkets. Soy yogurt is packaged the same way as other yogurt products and also can be found in the dairy case.

- **Silken-Style Tofu**
  Silken-style tofu, with its creamy, custard-like texture is an ideal ingredient to add to a smoothie. Silken tofu is rich in high-quality protein and is a good source of B-vitamins and iron. It is low in saturated fat and packed with fiber. Silken tofu can be found in the produce section of most supermarkets, or in the dairy or deli section. It is sold in water-filled tubs, vacuum-packed containers, or aseptic brick-shaped packages. Because it is ultra-pasteurized, it has a long shelf life, but once opened it should be refrigerated and used within three to four days.

- **Soy Dream Nondairy Frozen Dessert**
  Soy Dream is a nondairy and gluten-free frozen dessert made from soy milk. It is cholesterol-free, low in saturated fat, and has fewer calories than ordinary ice cream. It is available in the frozen section of most health food stores and some supermarkets.

- **Bee Pollen**
  This natural substance is rich in ordinary and essential amino acids, the building blocks of protein. Moreover, it contains 28 minerals, most of the known vitamins, 11 enzymes, and 14 fatty acids. All these nutrients, in just the right proportions, support the body's own healing and rejuvenation mechanisms, as well as increase energy, stamina, and endurance.

- **Ginkgo Biloba**
  This extract comes from the fan-shaped leaf of the ornamental ginkgo tree, a species that is reputed to be almost 200 million years old. The leaves are divided into two lobes, which accounts for the word *biloba* in the tree's name. Ginkgo biloba will not stop the aging process, but it is thought to increase blood flow to the brain, thereby enhancing several of its functions, and possibly lessening some of the symptoms of Alzheimer's disease, such as memory loss.

- **Ginseng**
  Another herb, many consider ginseng to be one of the best supplemental and restorative agents that nature provides. Among its attrib-

utes, it is reputed to increase mental alertness, restore vitality, relieve stress, and enhance immunity.

- **Flaxseed Oil**
  Flaxseed oil is rich in alpha-linolenic acid (ALA), an essential fatty acid used as a source of energy. ALA is a member of a healthful family of fats called omega-3 fatty acids. On the other hand, oils derived from corn, safflower, sesame, cottonseed, and sunflower are rich in less-healthful omega-6 fatty acids. It is important to keep a balance of omega-3 and omega-6 fatty acids in the diet to prevent health problems. Because American diets tend to be high in omega-6 fatty acids and low in omega-3 fatty acids, adding an omega-3 supplement such as flaxseed oil to your diet helps balance the two fatty acids.

- **Wheat Germ**
  Wheat germ is the germ or heart of the wheat kernel. This nutrition-packed food has a wonderful nutty flavor. Not only is it rich in insoluble fiber, but only 2 tablespoons provide 10 percent of the recommended daily allowance (RDA) of folate, zinc, and magnesium, and 15 percent of the RDA for vitamin E and thiamine.

- **Wheat Bran**
  Fiber is an important dietary constituent found in plant foods, such as vegetables, fruits, and grains. Bran, the outer part of grains, is richly endowed with fiber. Wheat bran has a

higher concentration of fiber than oat bran. Dietary fiber is divided into two categories: soluble fiber (found in such foods as oat bran, oatmeal, strawberries, and beans), and insoluble fiber (found in foods such as wheat bran, cauliflower, cabbage, and carrots). The American Heart Association recommends eating a diet that is low in saturated fat and cholesterol but rich in both soluble and insoluble fiber. Each form of fiber has specific health benefits. Soluble fiber in the diet helps lower blood cholesterol, while insoluble fiber plays an important role in maintaining normal bowel functions.

- **Protein Powders**
  Most often soy based, protein powders provide a natural source of amino acids, vitamins, minerals, fiber, and iron.

If you are craving instant low-cal refreshment that is satisfying and packed with nutrients, you need look no further than your own kitchen countertop. Simply add one or more power boosters, protein powders, or soybean products to your next smoothie and you can enjoy an energy-packed glassful that is as nutritious as it is delicious.

CHAPTER 2

The Lowdown on the Ingredients

How to Select, Prepare, and Store Fresh Fruit

Fresh fruits are the foundation of a smoothie. For this reason, being well-informed about the wide variety in this orchard bounty can be very helpful in your mission to create the perfect smoothie. This chapter will acquaint you with these delectable bundles of flavor and guide you in choosing, storing, and preparing them.

To begin with, it is important to realize that selecting smoothie-ready fruit may not be as easy as it looks, especially if your choice is based on appearance alone. At first glance, a peach may look ripe simply because of its rich color. However, there are a number of other less obvious attributes that are equally important. You should attempt to determine whether the fruit has a fresh aroma, how heavy or dense it is, and whether it is firm yet resilient to the touch. These characteristics are often more important than the fruit's color. The good news is that once you become a fruit connoisseur, you will find that it's actually quite easy to determine whether fruit is ripe.

I am certain that as you become more familiar with the wide array of fruit available, you will delight in the excitement of making deliciously refreshing smoothies. And the fact that a snack so satisfying can be so low in calories will amaze you. As you navigate the aisles of your favorite farmer's market or produce department, I hope you find the following fruitful information useful in your quest for the best nature has to offer.

APPLE

Apples are believed to have originated in central Asia and Caucasus, but they have been cultivated since prehistoric times. They were brought to the United States at the beginning of the seventeenth century, and later to Africa and Australia. Today, there are more than 100 varieties of apples commercially grown in the United States.

Apples—red, green, or yellow—all have a firm, crisp flesh. They are a rich source of fiber. Some apples have a sweet flavor with a hint of tartness, while others are less sweet and more tart. Most apples are delicious when made into a smoothie, but your flavor preference will determine the best variety for you.

Selection

When choosing an apple, look for one that is firm and crisp with a smooth, tight skin. Most important, the apple should have a sweet-smelling aroma. Avoid apples that have bruised or blemished skin. I recommend buying the organic variety whenever possible. Most nonorganic apples are heavily sprayed with pesticides and later waxed to preserve them and keep them looking fresh. Because organic apples have not been subjected to this treatment, you're more likely to find a worm here and there. But you can remove these unwelcome visitors when you cut the apple, thereby removing any health or aesthetic concerns. Wash in cool water and dry all apples well, organic or not. If you keep them separate from other fruit and vegetables, you can store apples in the crisper bin of the refrigerator for up to six weeks.

APRICOT

The apricot is a round or oblong fruit measuring about 2 inches in diameter with skin and flesh that is golden orange in color. It is a very sweet and juicy fruit with a single, smooth stone. The apricot is native to northern China and was eaten as early as 2200 B.C. Apricots are an excellent source of vitamins A and C, potassium, fiber, and iron.

Selection

When choosing apricots, look for those that are well colored, plump, and fairly firm but yield slightly when gently pressed. An apricot that is soft to the touch and juicy is fully ripe and should be eaten right away. If an apricot is hard, it can be placed in a brown paper bag and allowed to ripen at room temperature for a day or two. Avoid any that are green or yellow (these are not yet ripe). Refrigerate apricots in the crisper bin of the refrigerator for up to one week. Wash them in cool water just before using.

BANANA

The banana has been around for so long that, according to Hindu legend, it was actually the forbidden fruit in the garden of Eden. It also is believed that the banana was widely cultivated throughout Asia and Oceania before recorded history. Spanish colonists introduced banana shoots to the New World in 1516.

Bananas are reputed to be one of nature's best energy sources and are a rich source of vitamins A, B_6, and C, as well as fiber. They are ideal post-exercise fare because they replace important nutrients such as potassium, which is often lost during strenuous activity.

Selection

Bananas are picked when they are green and sweeten as they ripen. When choosing a banana, look for one that is completely yellow. The riper a banana, or the more yellow its skin, the sweeter it is. Bananas that are yellow but have green tips and green necks or those that are all yellow except for light green necks also are ready to eat. Green bananas will ripen at room temperature in two to three days. Alternatively, they can be placed in a brown paper bag to ripen. If a tomato or apple is added to the bag, the bananas will ripen even faster. A colorless gas called *ethylene* is produced within the cells of fruits, and stimulates ripening in many fruits and vegetables. When a banana is placed in the same bag with an apple or tomato, the ethylene from the apple or tomato will help ripen the banana. Once ripe, bananas can be stored at room temperature or in the refrigerator for a couple of days.

BLACKBERRY

The blackberry is a small black, blue, or dark red berry that grows on thorny bushes (brambles). These berries are oblong in shape and grow up to 1 inch in length. The United States is the world's dominant producer of blackberries. Blackberries are at their peak in flavor and availability from June through September, but may still be found in some supermarkets from November on into April. They are rich in vitamin C and fiber, and a good source of folate.

Selection

When choosing blackberries, look for ones that are plump and solid with full color and a bright, fresh appearance. Place them in a shallow container to prevent the berries on top from crushing those on the bottom. Cover the container and store it in the crisper bin of the refrigerator for one to two days. Wash blackberries in cool water just before using.

BLUEBERRY

Native to North America, the blueberry has the distinction of being the second most popular berry in the United States. It has been around for thousands of years, but not cultivated until the turn of the century. Today, 95 percent of the world's commercial crop of blueberries is grown in the United States. Blueberries reach their peak in flavor from mid-April to late September. They are available in the southern states first and gradually move north as the season progresses. Blueberries are an excellent source of vitamins A and C, as well as fiber.

Selection

When choosing blueberries, look for those that are plump and firm with a dark blue color and a silvery "bloom" (the powder on blueberries protects them from the sun—it does not rinse off). Avoid any that appear to be dull; this may indicate that the fruit is old. Blueberries should be prepared in the same way as blackberries, but they can be stored for a longer time in the crisper bin of the refrigerator, from three to five days.

CHERRY

Cherries are small, round, red to black fruit that grow on a tree. There are numerous varieties, but all of them fall into one of three categories: sweet, sour, or a hybrid of the two. Cherries grow in the temperate zones of Europe, Asia, and the Americas. It is believed that they originated in northeastern Asia and later spread throughout the temperate zones in prehistory, carried by birds that ate the cherries and later dropped the stones. Cherries are available from late May through early August. They are a good source of vitamin C and fiber.

Selection

When choosing cherries, look for those that are dark red, plump, and firm, with an attached stem. Store them in the crisper bin of the refrigerator for up to two days and wash them in cool water just before using.

KIWIFRUIT

The kiwifruit, about the size of a plum, grows on a vine. It has a brown fuzzy skin and a luscious sweet and sour emerald-green pulp that surrounds a cluster of black seeds. Kiwifruit originated in the 1600s in the Yangtze River valley in China where it was called *yangtao*. In 1906, yangtao seeds were sent to New Zealand, where the fruit was renamed Chinese gooseberry. In 1962, the Chinese gooseberry was shipped to the United States, where it was again renamed the kiwifruit in honor of New Zealand's famous national bird. Kiwifruit is available all year. It is high in vitamin C and fiber, and is a good source of vitamin E and potassium.

Selection

When choosing a kiwifruit, look for one that is light brown, has a sweet aroma, and feels firm yet will give slightly when pressed. Kiwifruit will ripen at room temperature in three to five days. You can also place kiwifruit in a brown paper bag, along with an apple or banana, to speed the ripening process. When ripe, store the kiwifruit in the crisper bin of the refrigerator for up to three weeks.

MANGO

Mangoes were cultivated in India and the Malay Archipelago as many as four thousand years ago. In the 1700s and 1800s, European explorers introduced the fruit to other tropical areas. Mangoes were first raised in the United States sometime in the early 1900s. The mango resembles a peach in appearance but is more elongated in shape. It has a thin, leathery skin that is waxy and smooth; its color can be green, red, orange, yellow, or any combination. The skin surrounds a very aromatic and juicy pulp and a hard inner pit. Mangoes are rich in beta-carotene, vitamin C, potassium, and fiber.

Selection

When choosing a mango, look for one that is very fragrant and plump around the stem area, and gives slightly when pressed. No matter what color they are when you buy them, the best-flavored mangoes will have a yellow tinge when ripe. Mangoes can be ripened at room temperature. To accelerate the process, place the mango and an apple in a brown paper bag overnight. Once ripened, mangoes can be stored in the crisper bin of the refrigerator for up to five days. Wash in cool water and dry the fruit well just before using.

MELON

Melons, surprisingly, are members of the cucumber family. They grow on vines that can reach up to 7 feet long. There are two distinct types of melons: muskmelons and watermelons. The muskmelon category includes summer melons (cantaloupe and muskmelon) and winter melons (casaba and honeydew). All melons are high in vitamin C.

Selection

When choosing a melon, look for one that is unblemished, firm, and free of any soft spots. Pick up a few melons and choose the one that is the heaviest for its size. Also, smell the stem end of the melon to see whether it has a fresh aroma of melon. If it has no aroma, the fruit is not ripe. To ripen a melon, place it in a loosely closed brown paper bag and let it sit at room temperature for two to three days. To speed up the ripening process, add a banana or an apple to the bag. When ripe, cut the melon into pieces and place the pieces in an airtight plastic bag. Store the melon in the refrigerator for up to three days.

ORANGE

Fresh oranges are grown widely in Florida, California, and Arizona and are available all year long. The two major varieties are the Valencia and the navel. Two other varieties grown in the western states are the cara cara and the Moro (a variety of blood orange), both of which are available throughout the winter months. Oranges are very high in vitamin C and fiber.

Selection

When selecting an orange, look for one that is heavy for its size, and firm. Avoid oranges with a bruised skin, indicating possible fermentation, as well as those with a loose skin, suggesting they may be dry inside. Although oranges can be stored at room temperature for a few days, refrigerating them is the best way to retain their flavor. Wash oranges in cool water before storing them in the crisper bin of the refrigerator.

PAPAYA

The papaya is native to North America and is cultivated in semitropical zones. It grows on trees that can reach heights of 20 feet, and the fruit itself can weigh 1 to 20 pounds. The most common variety grown in the United States, called the solo, flourishes in Hawaii and Florida. This pear-shaped fruit typically weighs up to 2 pounds and measures about 6 inches long. When ripe, the papaya has a distinctive golden-yellow skin. Its flesh, which is similar in color, is quite juicy and has a wonderful sweet–tart flavor. The center of the papaya is filled with dark, peppery seeds that are edible, but most people prefer to discard them.

Selection

When choosing a papaya, look for one with a skin that is rich, yellow-colored, smooth, and unblemished. It should emit a soft, fruity aroma and give slightly to palm pressure. It should also be heavy and symmetrical in shape. Avoid any with dark spots. A green papaya will ripen in two to three days at room temperature if placed in a brown paper bag. To accelerate the ripening process, place an apple or a banana in the bag with the papaya. Refrigerate completely ripe papayas for up to one week.

PEACH AND NECTARINE

Grown since prehistoric times, peaches were first cultivated in China. They were later introduced in Europe and Persia. It is believed that the Spaniards brought peaches to the Americas. The Spanish missionaries planted the first peach trees in California.

Numerous varieties of peaches are available, and they are broken down into rough classifications. One type of peach is the freestone, so named because the pit separates easily from the peach. Another variety is the clingstone, in which the pit is firmly attached to the fruit. The freestone is the peach most often found in supermarkets because it is easy to eat; clingstones are frequently canned. Peaches are available almost year-round and are a good source of vitamins A and C, as well as fiber.

The nectarine is a smooth-skinned variety of the peach. Nectarines are high in vitamin C, and rich in vitamin A and fiber.

Selection

When picking peaches, look for ones that are relatively firm with a fuzzy, creamy yellow skin, and a sweet aroma. The pink blush on the peach indicates its variety, not its ripeness. Avoid peaches with a wrinkled skin or those that are soft or blemished. The peach should yield slightly when touched. To ripen peaches, keep them at room temperature and out of direct sun until the skin yields slightly to the touch. Once ripe, store them in a single layer in the crisper bin of the refrigerator for up to five days. Wash peaches in cool water just before using.

When choosing nectarines, look for those with bright red markings over a yellow skin. Avoid any with wrinkled skin or those that are soft and bruised. The nectarine should yield slightly to the touch and have a sweet aroma. To ripen nectarines, place them in a brown paper bag and keep at room temperature. Once ripe, store them in a single layer in the crisper bin for up to one week. Wash nectarines in cool water just before using.

PEAR

The pear tree and its fruit are part of the rose family. It is believed that people ate pears as far back as the Stone Age. The pears we are accustomed to eating, however, were first cultivated in southeastern Europe and western Asia as "recently" as 2000 B.C. Pear trees were introduced to the Americas when European settlers arrived in the 1700s. Pears are a source of vitamin C, fiber, and potassium.

Selection

Pears are a unique fruit because they ripen best off the tree. This explains why they are often so hard when you buy them at the supermarket. Many pears have stickers that tell you the stage of ripeness, such as "Ready to eat" or "Let me ripen for two days." When choosing pears, look for ones that are firm and unblemished with a fresh pear aroma. To ripen pears, place them in a brown paper bag at room temperature for a few days. To speed up the ripening process, place a ripe banana or apple in the bag with the pear. When they yield to gentle thumb pressure, pears are ready to eat. Once ripe, wash pears in cool water and store them in the crisper bin of the refrigerator for two to five days.

PINEAPPLE

The pineapple is a tropical fruit that is native to Central and South America. In 1493, Christopher

Columbus discovered pineapples growing on the island of Guadeloupe and brought them back to Spain. By the 1700s, Europeans were growing pineapples in greenhouses throughout the continent. They are an excellent source of vitamin C.

Selection

When choosing a pineapple, look for one that has a fresh pineapple aroma and a crown with crisp, fresh-looking green leaves and a brightly colored shell. It should also be heavy and symmetrical in shape. Avoid any pineapples that are discolored or have soft spots. To store a pineapple, cut the fruit from the shell and refrigerate it in an airtight container for up to one week.

RASPBERRY

It is believed that red raspberries spread all over Europe and Asia in prehistoric times. Because wild raspberries were so delicious, it was not until the 1600s that Europeans began to cultivate them. Those that are cultivated in North America originated from two groups: the red raspberry, native to Europe, and the wild red variety, native to North America. Raspberries are an excellent source of vitamin C, fiber, and folate.

Selection

When choosing raspberries, it is always best to buy them when they are in season, which usually starts in late June and lasts four to six weeks. If you are fortunate enough to have a local berry farm, take advantage of it by visiting at the beginning of the season to get the best pick. Select berries that are large and plump, uniform in color, and free of mold. Avoid any that are mushy. Before refrigerating raspberries, carefully go through the batch and discard any that show signs of spoilage. Place the raspberries in a shallow container to prevent the berries on top from crushing those on the bottom. Cover the container and store it in the crisper bin of the refrigerator for one to two days. Wash raspberries in cool water just before you are ready to use them.

STRAWBERRY

Strawberries date as far back as 2,200 years ago. They are known to have grown wild in Italy in the third century, and by 1588, they were discovered in Virginia by the first European settlers. Local Indians cultivated the strawberry as early as the mid-1600s and by the middle of the nineteenth century, this fruit was widely grown in many parts of North America.

The strawberry grows in groups of three on the stem of a plant that is very low to the ground. As the fruit ripens, it changes from greenish white in color to a lush flame red. The strawberry does not have a skin; it is actually covered by hundreds of tiny seeds. Strawberries are a rich source of vitamin C and fiber.

Selection

The best time to buy strawberries is in June and July when they are at their peak of juicy freshness. As with raspberries, if you are lucky enough to live near a strawberry farm, a "pick your own" day trip is a wonderful family outing as well as an excellent way to get the very best of the crop. Look for plump, firm, and deeply colored fruit with a bright green cap and a sweet strawberry aroma. Strawberries can be stored in a single layer in the crisper bin of the refrigerator for up to two days. Wash them with their caps in cool water just before you are ready to use them.

FREEZING FRUIT

To give your smoothies the optimal consistency, it is important that you freeze the fresh fruit for 30 minutes or more before using it. This also helps maintain the smoothie's ideal icy cold temperature.

You may also want to freeze fruit to store it for later use. This is especially useful when you know that certain seasonal fruits will no longer be available after a certain date. By purchasing an ample quantity to freeze, you can be certain of having a supply on hand when you need it to prepare one of your favorite smoothies. Also, there may be times when you don't need ripened fruit immediately; freezing prevents overripening and allows you to use it at your leisure.

Whether you are getting fruit ready to freeze for tomorrow morning's smoothie or for sometime next week, the basic preparation is the same.

- When ready to freeze **cherries** and **apricots** (which should be cut in half and their stones removed) or **berries,** place them in a colander and rinse with a gentle stream of cool water. Pat them dry with a paper towel.

- To freeze a **peach, nectarine** (remove its stone), or **pear** (remove its stem and seeds), cut them into small pieces.

- For a **banana** or **kiwifruit,** remove the skin and either slice it or freeze it whole and slice it later, just before using.

- Before freezing **oranges,** remove the peel and pith, break each into segments, and remove any seeds.

- To prepare **apples, mangoes, melons,** and **papayas** for freezing, remove their peels and seeds or pits, then cube.

- When ready to freeze a **pineapple,** remove its top, the outer skin, and the core, then cut into cubes.

Place prepared fruit on a baking sheet lined with freezer paper, plastic coated side facing up. In a pinch, you may use waxed paper or parchment paper instead. Freeze the fruit for 30 minutes or longer, after which time it will be ready to add to the other smoothie ingredients. If frozen fruit is to be used at a later date, transfer the frozen pieces to an airtight plastic bag large enough to hold them in a single layer. Label and mark the date on the bag, and freeze for up to two weeks. Most fruit can be kept in the freezer this long without losing flavor.

HOW MUCH FRUIT SHOULD I BUY?

To determine how much fruit you need to make a smoothie, the list that follows provides an estimate of the quantity of fruit you get once the skin, hull, seeds, pit, and core are removed. You can use the average weight per individual fruit provided in the table, or to be more precise, you can weigh the fruit, using the supermarket scale, before purchase.

Fruit	How Much to Buy	Average Weight	Number of Cups
Apple	1 medium	6 ounces	1 cup
Apricots	3	8 ounces	1 cup
Banana	1 large	10 ounces	1 cup
Blackberries	½ pint	6 ounces	1¼ cups
Blueberries	½ pint	8 ounces	1 cup
Cantaloupe	1 medium	3 pounds	5 cups
Cherries	20	8 ounces	1 cup
Kiwifruit	3	8 ounces	1 cup
Mango	1 medium	10 ounces	1 cup
Nectarine	1 medium	8 ounces	1 cup
Orange	1 medium	10 ounces	1 cup

(continues)

(continued from page 25)

Fruit	How Much to Buy	Average Weight	Number of Cups
Papaya	1 medium	10 ounces	1 cup
Peach	1 medium	8 ounces	1 cup
Pear	1 medium	6 ounces	1 cup
Pineapple	1 medium	3 pounds	5½ cups
Raspberries	1 box	6 ounces	1¼ cups
Strawberries	7 to 8 medium	6 ounces	1 cup

CHAPTER 3

Let's Get Started

Equipment and Techniques for Making a Slim Smoothie

The popularity of smoothies is largely due to their nutritional benefits and great taste, but for many of us with a busy lifestyle, their ease of preparation also gets two thumbs up. When dieting, finding the time to prepare special foods that are both low in calories and fat *and* healthful can be a challenge. Yet you can prepare a smoothie, made of the simplest ingredients, in just minutes. With a little planning, and with minimal effort, you can blend a satisfying and richly flavored low-calorie treat any time of the day. With such an unbeatable combination of good taste and ease of preparation, it is no wonder that smoothies have quickly become one of the culinary rages of our era.

You will be pleased to learn that an extensive array of equipment isn't necessary to create this miracle of flavors in a glass. In fact, all you need to outfit your smoothie station is a modest assortment of essential tools: a sharp knife for prepping fruit, a rubber spatula to remove every last drop from the blender, airtight freezer bags for storing freshly cut fruit in the freezer, and, of course, the essential blender.

There are a few optional items you might want to consider. As you glance through the garnish recipes found in this book, you will note that some suggest using a silicone mat—a reusable laminated food-grade silicone sheet that prevents food from sticking during the baking process. This is a very useful item, but not an absolute necessity. Finally, although a food processor can be used to make a smoothie, most smoothie experts prefer their trusty blenders. Pureeing fruit and ice in a food processor, for example, often leaves small chunks of ice. On the other hand, a blender breaks up the ice and fruit into tiny particles and does a better job processing liquids and solids into a fine, smooth, and well-aerated purée.

EQUIPMENT

The blender is by far the most important piece of kitchen equipment you will need to make a proper smoothie. The invention of this indispensable appliance is credited to Stephen J. Poplawski who, in 1922, first conceived of placing a spinning blade at the bottom of a glass container. By 1935, Fred Waring and Frederick Osius made significant improvements on the original design and began marketing the Waring blender. The rest is history.

A blender basically consists of a tall and narrow stainless steel, plastic, or glass food container fitted with metal blades at the bottom. These blades usually have four cutting edges placed on two or four planes allowing for the ingredients in the container to hit multiple cutting surfaces. The rapidly spinning blades cause an upward motion, creating a vortex in the container that allows for the incorporation of more air in the final product, giving it a smoother consistency.

When selecting a blender, you should assess certain basic qualities, including its durability, ease of operation and cleaning, capacity, and noise production. With such a wide variety of blenders from which to choose, I hope the following information will help you narrow your choice.

- Blender containers typically come in two sizes: 32 ounces and 40 ounces. If you will routinely be preparing smoothies for more than two people, choose the larger size.

- Blender motors come in different sizes. Those with 290-watt motors are adequate for most blending jobs, but not optimal for smoothies. Others with 330- to 400-watt motors are considered to be of professional caliber and are excellent for crushing ice, a feature that is very important for creating the best smoothies.

- Blenders can be found with a variety of blade speed options, ranging from just two speeds (high and low) to multiple (between five and fourteen) speeds. Variable-speed models provide more options, such as the ability to liquefy and whip.

- The blender should have a removable bottom for easier cleaning.

- Container lids should have a secondary, removable lid. This allows you to add ingredients while the blender is turned on.

- Avoid plastic container jars because they get scratched over time and do not stand up well in the dishwasher.

Recently, a new blender designed specifically to make smoothies has hit the market. This whirring wizard, called the Smoothie Elite (by Back to Basics), has several unique features, including a custom stir stick to break up the air pockets, an ice-crunching blade that ensures consistent smoothie texture, and a convenient spigot at the bottom of the container that serves up the finished product.

Although a blender is the ideal appliance for making smoothies, you may prefer a food processor because of its overall versatility, or more importantly, because it is an appliance that you already own. *The New York Times* described the food processor as the "twentieth-century French revolution." This appliance can mince, chop, grate, shred, slice, knead, blend, purée, liquefy, and crush ice.

The food processor has a base directly under the work bowl that houses the motor. A metal shaft extending from the base through the center of the work bowl connects the blade or disc to the motor. A cover that fits over the work bowl has a feed tube. When the bowl is locked into place and the motor is switched on, the shaft turns and propels the blades or discs. Unlike the blender container, the food processor bowl is wide and low, causing food to be sent sideways rather than upward by the spinning blade. This motion results in food striking the sides of the container, with less incorporation of air than in the upward motion produced by a blender.

Similar to the blender, the food processor has some basic features you should assess when selecting the one that will best fit your cooking needs.

- Food processors come in a wide range of sizes. The 2- or 3-cup miniprocessor is practical for chopping, especially small quantities of food. Those with 7-, 9-, and 11-cup capacities are each equally suitable for making smoothies, as well as other food preparations, while 14- and 20-cup units are ideal for professional cooking needs.

- Although a few food processors have four speeds, most have two: high and low, in addition to a pulsing action.

- Some food processors come with both large and small feed tubes. The larger tube is convenient when large-sized ingredients are to be added while the machine is running.

Once you have decided on the features you would like in a blender (or food processor), I encourage you to visit several appliance or department stores and view the various models available. The salesclerk should be able to provide you with any additional information you need to make the best decision. You can also do appliance research on the Internet. Many of the companies that manufacture these appliances have sites that are quite informative about their individual products, and some also provide a phone number so you can speak to a representative. Finally, *Consumer Reports* and similar publications provide comparison quality ratings for a variety of blenders and food processors.

HELPFUL TECHNIQUES

Now that the blender has taken its rightful place, center stage on your countertop, it is time to rev it up and make a smoothie. Equipping your kitchen with the necessary tools to make smoothies was relatively easy, and you will be pleased to learn that mastering the techniques required to prepare them is just as simple. In fact, preparing a smoothie may be one of the most uncomplicated tasks you will ever do in your kitchen. Simply place all the smoothie ingredients in the blender, and you will end up with a perfectly acceptable final product. However, for those who want to create the ultimate smoothie, I have discovered a few techniques that will help you reach that lofty goal:

- To get the most delicious fruit, buy it when it is in season and at its peak in flavor.

- Before freezing fruit, wash and dry it first, and then follow the preparation instructions given in chapter 2.

- When ready to freeze the fruit, set it in a shallow pan lined with a piece of freezer paper, plastic-coated side facing up to prevent it from sticking to the surface. In a pinch, you may use waxed paper or parchment paper instead. Place the fruit in the freezer for at least 30 minutes or until partially frozen. Using frozen fruit ensures that the smoothie will have a thick consistency and be icy cold.

- Store-bought individually frozen fruit can be substituted for fresh frozen fruit, but it should be used within six months of the purchase date. Avoid using frozen fruit that is packaged in sweetened syrup.

- To be certain that you have a supply of your favorite seasonal fruits, stock up before they are no longer available for purchase. Although fruits have the most flavor when kept frozen for one to two weeks, they can be kept in the freezer slightly longer if necessary.

- If using ice in a smoothie, ice pieces should be slightly smaller than the cut-up fruit to prevent any chunks of ice remaining once the smoothie is blended. If you don't own a high-speed blender, you will have to make your own crushed ice by placing ice cubes in a resealable bag and crushing them with a mallet or rolling pin. An easier alternative to cutting the ice is to buy a bag of ice chips or crushed ice to keep in your freezer.

- Fill mini ice cube trays with orange, lemon, lime, pineapple, or apple juice to create frozen juice cubes. Substituting these for some or all of the plain cubes in a smoothie will add additional fruity flavor to the drink.

- If the fruit you have frozen becomes clumped together, gently pound the clumps within the sealed bag with a mallet or blunt object until the pieces have separated.

- When adding ingredients to a blender, always add the chilled liquid first, then the frozen fruit, and the ice or frozen yogurt last. Start the blender on low speed to crush the ice and fruit and blend the mixture. Gradually increase the speed until the mixture is smooth. It takes three to four minutes for a smoothie to reach its optimal consistency. It may be necessary to turn the blender off periodically and stir the mixture with a spoon, working from the bottom up.

- If the smoothie is too thin, add more fruit or ice. Conversely, if the smoothie is too thick, add more liquid.

CHAPTER 4

Sleek and Simple Smoothies

Smoothies are one of the most celebrated and refreshing taste treats to have emerged in recent years. The most basic variety of these cool creations, like the recipes in this chapter, can be made with a simple combination of fresh fruits and juices. They are a healthy, lowfat, and delicious alternative to more fat- and calorie-laden blended drinks, such as malts, milk shakes, and blizzards.

In creating these recipes, I was guided by the understanding that the calorie count in even the most basic smoothies can ratchet up deceptively unless you pay careful attention to the ingredients. As you glance at these smoothie recipes, notice that bananas are used frequently. This is because they provide just the right amount of sweetness and texture. Depending on its size, a single banana can have as many as 100 to 120 calories.

If you are on a very restricted diet, you should consider substituting fruits that have even fewer calories than a banana, such as melon or strawberries. The variety of juice used can also affect the calorie count. Most fruit nectars are higher in calories than simple juices. Although nectars add rich flavor to a smoothie, you'll still be pleased with the delicious results when you use unsweetened apple or peach juice instead. The naturally low-cal and lowfat pleasures found in this chapter deserve one more kudos: With every swallow you are well on your way to fulfilling the American Cancer Institute's recommendation to include at least two to three servings of fruit in your daily diet.

As you browse through this chapter, you will be impressed with the variety of fruit and juice combinations, which are limited only by your imagination. Get ready to be impressed when you try Dole-Licious (page 45), a refreshing smoothie featuring pineapple blended with banana and apple juice. If you're a mango devotee, then you will be thrilled with the taste of Man-goooooooooooooal! (page 73), a delicious blend of mango, pineapple, mango juice, and mango sorbet.

As you prepare the recipes in this chapter, I hope you will feel inspired to experiment with some of your own favorite fruit and juice combinations. Now that you know some of my smoothie secrets, use them and then pass them on!

SUPER LOW-CAL SMOOTHIES

These smoothies have 250 or fewer calories.

Shopping List

Fruit

Apricots
Bananas
Blackberries
Blueberries
Cantaloupe
Cherries
Mangos
Oranges
Papayas
Peaches
Pineapple
Raspberries
Strawberries
Tangerines (or
    clementines)

Juice

Orange juice
Unsweetened apple
    juice
Unsweetened guava
    juice
Unsweetened mango
    juice
Unsweetened peach
    juice
Unsweetened pine-
    apple juice
White cranberry juice

Miscellaneous

Honey (optional)
Raspberry sorbet
Strawberry sorbet

Be Berry, Berry Quiet

You're going to have to fight the temptation to shout from the rooftops about this low-calorie, high-flavor raspberry smoothie. This bit of refreshment in a glass is the perfect smoothie to share with friends after a workout at the gym.

1 SERVING

½ cup unsweetened peach juice

1 to 2 teaspoons honey (or to taste), optional

1 cup raspberries

½ cup diced banana

¼ cup raspberry sorbet

Place all ingredients in a blender and mix by using the on/off pulse function until the ingredients are mostly blended. Continue mixing, gradually increasing the speed, until the mixture is smooth. Pour the smoothie into a glass and garnish with Berries on a Skewer (page 199), if desired.

Calories	249	Calcium	32 mg
Calories from fat	9	Iron	1 mg
Total fat	1 g	Potassium	512 mg
Carbohydrates	62 g	Beta-carotene	84 mcg
Protein	2 g	Magnesium	44 mg
Fiber	11 g	Folic Acid	46 mcg

Berry Manilow

*If you're "Ready to Take a Chance Again" with a
new kind of taste treat, then "This One's for You."
Made with blueberries, papaya, and banana, it's
the ultimate treat to serve the next time you invite
friends over for a karaoke party.*

1 SERVING

½ cup unsweetened guava juice

1 to 2 teaspoons honey (or to taste), optional

½ cup blueberries

½ cup diced papaya

½ cup diced banana

Place all ingredients in a blender and mix by
using the on/off pulse function until the ingredients are mostly blended. Continue mixing, gradually increasing the speed, until the mixture is
smooth. Pour the smoothie into a glass and garnish with Melon Balls on a Skewer (page 204), if
desired.

Calories	186	Calcium	51 mg
Calories from fat	9	Iron	1 mg
Total fat	1 g	Potassium	477 mg
Carbohydrates	47 g	Beta Carotene	71 mcg
Protein	2 g	Magnesium	29 mg
Fiber	6 g	Folic Acid	41 mcg

Ber-ry Market

There is no overselling how spectacular this berry-laden smoothie is. It may be "short" on calories, but it's rich in flavors. One taste and you'll understand why this tempting glassful has such a favorable praise-to-yearning ratio.

1 SERVING

½ cup orange juice

1 to 2 teaspoons honey (or to taste), optional

½ cup diced banana

¼ cup blueberries

¼ cup raspberries

¼ cup diced strawberries

Place all ingredients in a blender and mix by using the on/off pulse function until the ingredients are mostly blended. Continue mixing, gradually increasing the speed, until the mixture is smooth. Pour the smoothie into a glass and garnish the rim with a Strawberry Fan (page 211), if desired.

Calories	166	Calcium	40 mg
Calories from fat	11	Iron	1 mg
Total fat	1 g	Potassium	655 mg
Carbohydrates	41 g	Beta Carotene	100 mcg
Protein	2 g	Magnesium	45 mg
Fiber	7 g	Folic Acid	66 mcg

Black & White

There is only one way to look at it: Either you're on a diet or you're not. Either way, this blackberry and banana smoothie gets high marks for being a deliciously sweet, low-calorie treat. Enjoy this delightful smoothie whenever you crave something sweet and satisfying.

1 SERVING

½ cup unsweetened apple juice

1 to 2 teaspoons honey (or to taste), optional

1 cup blackberries

½ cup diced banana

Place all ingredients in a blender and mix by using the on/off pulse function until the ingredients are mostly blended. Continue mixing, gradually increasing the speed, until the mixture is smooth. Pour the smoothie into a glass and garnish with an Apple Chip (page 195), if desired.

Calories	202	Calcium	59 mg
Calories from fat	10	Iron	2 mg
Total fat	1 g	Potassium	727 mg
Carbohydrates	50 g	Beta Carotene	106 mcg
Protein	2 g	Magnesium	54 mg
Fiber	10 g	Folic Acid	63 mcg

Cherry Potter

Owl deliver a special invitation to you to try this unforgettable cherry, pineapple, and banana smoothie. Invite friends over to watch movies and share this magical treat.

1 SERVING

½ cup unsweetened pineapple juice

1 to 2 teaspoons honey (or to taste), optional

1 cup diced cherries

½ cup diced pineapple

¼ cup diced banana

Place all ingredients in a blender and mix by using the on/off pulse function until the ingredients are mostly blended. Continue mixing, gradually increasing the speed, until the mixture is smooth. Pour the smoothie into a glass and garnish the rim with an Orange, Lemon, and Cherry Combo (page 206), if desired.

Calories	247	Calcium	51 mg
Calories from fat	18	Iron	1 mg
Total fat	2 g	Potassium	728 mg
Carbohydrates	60 g	Beta Carotene	199 mcg
Protein	3 g	Magnesium	54 mg
Fiber	5 g	Folic Acid	50 mcg

Cran Central Station

You'll be on track to eliminate that caboose with this first-class, low-cal cranberry refresher.

1 SERVING

½ cup white cranberry juice

1 to 2 teaspoons honey (or to taste), optional

½ cup diced cantaloupe

½ cup blackberries

½ cup diced pineapple

Place all ingredients in a blender and mix by using the on/off pulse function until the ingredients are mostly blended. Continue mixing, gradually increasing the speed, until the mixture is smooth. Pour the smoothie into a glass and garnish with a Pineapple Bow (page 207), if desired.

Calories	157	Calcium	37 mg
Calories from fat	7	Iron	1 mg
Total fat	1 g	Potassium	470 mg
Carbohydrates	38 g	Beta Carotene	1541 mcg
Protein	2 g	Magnesium	34 mg
Fiber	5 g	Folic Acid	46 mcg

Darlin' Clementine

No need to be dreadful sorry after enjoying a glass-ful of this low-cal smoothie containing tangerines (also called clementines). Serve this tangy concoction as part of a nutritious breakfast, or any time you crave a filling and satisfying refreshment.

1 SERVING

½ cup orange juice

1 to 2 teaspoons honey (or to taste), optional

1½ cups diced tangerine (or clementine),
   seeds removed

½ cup diced banana

Place all ingredients in a blender and mix by using the on/off pulse function until the ingredients are mostly blended. Continue mixing, gradually increasing the speed, until the mixture is smooth. Pour the smoothie into a glass and garnish the rim with an Orange Wheel (page 203), if desired.

Calories	250	Calcium	59 mg
Calories from fat	10	Iron	1 mg
Total fat	1 g	Potassium	1004 mg
Carbohydrates	63 g	Beta Carotene	1697 mcg
Protein	3 g	Magnesium	70 mg
Fiber	9 g	Folic Acid	110 mcg

Dole-Licious

See if you don't agree that this tantalizing smoothie, infused with pineapple and banana, doesn't deserve an exclamation mark!

1 SERVING

½ cup unsweetened apple juice

1 to 2 teaspoons honey (or to taste), optional

1 cup diced pineapple

½ cup diced banana

Place all ingredients in a blender and mix by using the on/off pulse function until the ingredients are mostly blended. Continue mixing, gradually increasing the speed, until the mixture is smooth. Pour the smoothie into a glass and garnish the rim with a Pineapple Wedge (page 208), if desired.

Calories	203	Calcium	24 mg
Calories from fat	10	Iron	1 mg
Total fat	1 g	Potassium	620 mg
Carbohydrates	51 g	Beta Carotene	55 mcg
Protein	1 g	Magnesium	47 mg
Fiber	4 g	Folic Acid	31 mcg

Five Easy Peaches

You don't have to start the morning with a glass-ful of this low-calorie taste sensation, but after one sip of this peach-filled smoothie, you'll discover there are no substitutions for its great taste.

1 SERVING

½ cup orange juice

1 to 2 teaspoons honey (or to taste), optional

1 cup diced peach

½ cup diced mango

Place all ingredients in a blender and mix by using the on/off pulse function until the ingredients are mostly blended. Continue mixing, gradually increasing the speed, until the mixture is smooth. Pour the smoothie into a glass and garnish the rim with a Lime Wheel (page 203), if desired.

Calories	183	Calcium	30 mg
Calories from fat	6	Iron	1 mg
Total fat	1 g	Potassium	712 mg
Carbohydrates	46 g	Beta Carotene	2423 mcg
Protein	2 g	Magnesium	33 mg
Fiber	5 g	Folic Acid	54 mcg

Go Man-Go

This mango and banana smoothie is soooooo cool in more ways than one! Serve this refreshing fruit combination after a day at the gym.

1 SERVING

½ cup unsweetened mango juice

1 to 2 teaspoons honey (or to taste), optional

1 cup diced banana

½ cup diced mango

Place all ingredients in a blender and mix by using the on/off pulse function until the ingredients are mostly blended. Continue mixing, gradually increasing the speed, until the mixture is smooth. Pour the smoothie into a glass and garnish with a Banana Wafer (page 197), if desired.

Calories	250	Calcium	67 mg
Calories from fat	8	Iron	1 mg
Total fat	1 g	Potassium	723 mg
Carbohydrates	64 g	Beta Carotene	1998 mcg
Protein	97 g	Magnesium	51 mg
Fiber	6 g	Folic Acid	40 mcg

Mango Mania

Is it any wonder that everyone starts raving when they taste this sensational mango smoothie? Share the enthusiasm with your family by making up a pitcherful of this dieter's dream come true.

1 SERVING

½ cup unsweetened mango juice

1 to 2 teaspoons honey (or to taste), optional

1 cup diced mango

½ cup diced cherries

Place all ingredients in a blender and mix by using the on/off pulse function until the ingredients are mostly blended. Continue mixing, gradually increasing the speed, until the mixture is smooth. Pour the smoothie into a glass and garnish with a Pineapple Bow (page 207), if desired.

Calories	219	Calcium	77 mg
Calories from fat	10	Iron	1 mg
Total fat	1 g	Potassium	420 mg
Carbohydrates	55 g	Beta Carotene	3935 mcg
Protein	97 g	Magnesium	23 mg
Fiber	5 g	Folic Acid	26 mcg

Mano a Mango

See if you can face up to the challenge of putting the glass down after only one serving of this pleasingly sweet smoothie packed with the wonderful flavors of mango, orange, and banana.

1 SERVING

½ cup orange juice

1 to 2 teaspoons honey (or to taste), optional

1 cup diced mango

½ cup diced banana

Place all ingredients in a blender and mix by using the on/off pulse function until the ingredients are mostly blended. Continue mixing, gradually increasing the speed, until the mixture is smooth. Pour the smoothie into a glass and garnish with Mint Leaves (page 205), if desired.

Calories	232	Calcium	35 mg
Calories from fat	9	Iron	1 mg
Total fat	1 g	Potassium	802 mg
Carbohydrates	59 g	Beta Carotene	3933 mcg
Protein	2 g	Magnesium	50 mg
Fiber	5 g	Folic Acid	75 mcg

Melon Rouge

Whether you're a left-bank person or a right-bank person, you'll agree that the deep golden-orange color of this tantalizing smoothie is certainly an "Eiffel." Share this satiny smoothie with friends while lounging around the pool.

1 SERVING

½ cup orange juice

1 to 2 teaspoons honey (or to taste), optional

1½ cups diced cantaloupe

¼ cup diced banana

Place all ingredients in a blender and mix by using the on/off pulse function until the ingredients are mostly blended. Continue mixing, gradually increasing the speed, until the mixture is smooth. Pour the smoothie into a glass and garnish with Melon Balls on a Skewer (page 204), if desired.

Calories	172	Calcium	42 mg
Calories from fat	10	Iron	1 mg
Total fat	1 g	Potassium	1120 mg
Carbohydrates	41 g	Beta Carotene	4557 mcg
Protein	3 g	Magnesium	50 mg
Fiber	3 g	Folic Acid	84 mcg

My Blueberry Heaven

Start the day by serving this heavenly tasting blue-berry, mango, and banana smoothie to your family and it's certain to put angelic smiles on their faces. Serve with a lowfat blueberry bagel.

1 SERVING

½ cup orange juice

1 to 2 teaspoons honey (or to taste), optional

½ cup blueberries

½ cup diced mango

½ cup diced banana

Place all ingredients in a blender and mix by using the on/off pulse function until the ingredients are mostly blended. Continue mixing, gradually increasing the speed, until the mixture is smooth. Pour the smoothie into a glass and garnish with Berries on a Skewer (page 199), if desired.

Calories	208	Calcium	46 mg
Calories from fat	12	Iron	1 mg
Total fat	1 g	Potassium	674 mg
Carbohydrates	53 g	Beta Carotene	2008 mcg
Protein	3 g	Magnesium	43 mg
Fiber	7 g	Folic Acid	63 mcg

Picablue Treat

After a day on the slopes, enjoy a super giant glass-ful of this blueberry and banana smoothie, and the rest of your meal will be all downhill. Serve with an assortment of lowfat berry muffins.

1 SERVING

½ cup unsweetened apple juice

1 to 2 teaspoons honey (or to taste), optional

1 cup blueberries

½ cup diced banana

Place all ingredients in a blender and mix by using the on/off pulse function until the ingredients are mostly blended. Continue mixing, gradually increasing the speed, until the mixture is smooth. Pour the smoothie into a glass and garnish with an Apple Chip (page 195), if desired.

Calories	187	Calcium	53 mg
Calories from fat	13	Iron	1 mg
Total fat	2 g	Potassium	445 mg
Carbohydrates	49 g	Beta Carotene	37 mcg
Protein	2 g	Magnesium	25 mg
Fiber	8 g	Folic Acid	14 mcg

Return to Slender

Put your own stamp on a diet that works. Start with this low-calorie strawberry and banana smoothie that really delivers. For an added treat, serve with a bowl of strawberries lightly dusted with a hint of powdered sugar.

1 SERVING

½ cup unsweetened apple juice

1 to 2 teaspoons honey (or to taste), optional

¾ cup diced banana

½ cup diced strawberries

¼ cup strawberry sorbet

Place all ingredients in a blender and mix by using the on/off pulse function until the ingredients are mostly blended. Continue mixing, gradually increasing the speed, until the mixture is smooth. Pour the smoothie into a glass and garnish the rim with a Strawberry Fan (page 211), if desired.

Calories	250	Calcium	26 mg
Calories from fat	9	Iron	1 mg
Total fat	1 g	Potassium	719 mg
Carbohydrates	63 g	Beta Carotene	67 mcg
Protein	2 g	Magnesium	44 mg
Fiber	5 g	Folic Acid	35 mcg

Skinny the Blue

If you can't Bear the thought of those few extra pounds, don't Pooh Pooh this opportunity to lose them and enjoy the delicious taste combination of strawberries, blueberries, and bananas.

1 SERVING

½ cup white cranberry juice

1 to 2 teaspoons honey (or to taste), optional

½ cup diced strawberries

½ cup blueberries

½ cup diced banana

Place all ingredients in a blender and mix by using the on/off pulse function until the ingredients are mostly blended. Continue mixing, gradually increasing the speed, until the mixture is smooth. Pour the smoothie into a glass and garnish with Berries on a Skewer (page 199), if desired.

Calories	176	Calcium	35 mg
Calories from fat	10	Iron	1 mg
Total fat	1 g	Potassium	423 mg
Carbohydrates	44 g	Beta Carotene	48 mcg
Protein	2 g	Magnesium	29 mg
Fiber	7 g	Folic Acid	28 mcg

Skinny Sipping

Take it off. Take it all off—pounds that is—with this ultra-low-calorie combination of flavorful fruit with a touch of honey. Invite friends over for a pool party and serve this sensational smoothie.

1 SERVING

½ cup unsweetened pineapple juice

1 to 2 teaspoons honey (or to taste), optional

½ cup diced cantaloupe

½ cup diced peach

½ cup diced pineapple

Place all ingredients in a blender and mix by using the on/off pulse function until the ingredients are mostly blended. Continue mixing, gradually increasing the speed, until the mixture is smooth. Pour the smoothie into a glass and garnish the rim with a Pineapple Slice (page 208), if desired.

Calories	172	Calcium	40 mg
Calories from fat	7	Iron	1 mg
Total fat	1 g	Potassium	664 mg
Carbohydrates	43 g	Beta Carotene	1736 mcg
Protein	2 g	Magnesium	42 mg
Fiber	4 g	Folic Acid	53 mcg

Sleek to Sleek

You'll be in heaven after one taste of this cherry, banana, and peach smoothie. Because it is so low in calories, you can savor this taste sensation as a healthful addition to a meal or an in-between snack.

1 SERVING

½ cup unsweetened apple juice

1 to 2 teaspoons honey (or to taste), optional

½ cup diced cherries

½ cup diced banana

½ cup diced peach

Place all ingredients in a blender and mix by using the on/off pulse function until the ingredients are mostly blended. Continue mixing, gradually increasing the speed, until the mixture is smooth. Pour the smoothie into a glass and garnish the rim with an Orange, Lemon, and Cherry Combo (page 206), if desired.

Calories	216	Calcium	28 mg
Calories from fat	11	Iron	1 mg
Total fat	1 g	Potassium	774 mg
Carbohydrates	54 g	Beta Carotene	346 mcg
Protein	2 g	Magnesium	39 mg
Fiber	5 g	Folic Acid	20 mcg

Slender Bender

It's no accident that this strawberry, banana, and apricot smoothie, jolted with a dash of strawberry sorbet, tastes so smashingly delicious.

1 SERVING

½ cup unsweetened pineapple juice

1 to 2 teaspoons honey (or to taste), optional

½ cup diced strawberries

⅓ cup diced banana

½ cup diced apricots

¼ cup strawberry sorbet

Place all ingredients in a blender and mix by using the on/off pulse function until the ingredients are mostly blended. Continue mixing, gradually increasing the speed, until the mixture is smooth. Pour the smoothie into a glass and garnish the rim with a Strawberry Fan (page 211), if desired.

Calories	223	Calcium	44 mg
Calories from fat	7	Iron	1 mg
Total fat	1 g	Potassium	622 mg
Carbohydrates	54 g	Beta Carotene	1235 mcg
Protein	2 g	Magnesium	38 mg
Fiber	5 g	Folic Acid	54 mcg

Slender Trap

You'll get hooked on this flavorful mango, banana, and orange smoothie after just one taste. Serve this seductively delicious smoothie while lounging on the patio on a starry night.

1 SERVING

½ cup unsweetened apple juice

1 to 2 teaspoons honey (or to taste), optional

½ cup diced mango

½ cup diced banana

½ cup diced orange

Place all ingredients in a blender and mix by using the on/off pulse function until the ingredients are mostly blended. Continue mixing, gradually increasing the speed, until the mixture is smooth. Pour the smoothie into a glass and garnish the rim with an Orange Wheel (page 203), if desired.

Calories	223	Calcium	57 mg
Calories from fat	7	Iron	1 mg
Total fat	1 g	Potassium	736 mg
Carbohydrates	57 g	Beta Carotene	1997 mcg
Protein	2 g	Magnesium	42 mg
Fiber	6 g	Folic Acid	53 mcg

Supercalorierestricted getsmewellindoses

Just Poppin your blender some apricot, banana, and mango, along with a spoonful of honey, and watch how easily this delightfully healthful smoothie goes down. It's the perfect refreshment to offer when having friends over to watch movie classics. Serve this delectable concoction along with a plateful of your favorite sugar-free cookies.

1 SERVING

½ cup unsweetened apple juice

1 to 2 teaspoons honey (or to taste), optional

½ cup diced apricots

½ cup diced mango

½ cup diced banana

Place all ingredients in a blender and mix by using the on/off pulse function until the ingredients are mostly blended. Continue mixing, gradually increasing the speed, until the mixture is smooth. Pour the smoothie into a glass and garnish with an Apple Chip (page 195), if desired.

Calories	218	Calcium	32 mg
Calories from fat	9	Iron	1 mg
Total fat	1 g	Potassium	803 mg
Carbohydrates	55 g	Beta Carotene	3169 mcg
Protein	2 g	Magnesium	39 mg
Fiber	5 g	Folic Acid	33 mcg

Thin One for the Sipper

Your family and friends will cheer when they "first down" a glassful of this low-calorie refresher. You don't have to be Irish to enjoy this delightful mixture, so don't pass on the opportunity.

1 SERVING

½ cup unsweetened apple juice

1 to 2 teaspoons honey (or to taste), optional

½ cup diced apricots

½ cup diced mango

½ cup blueberries

Place all ingredients in a blender and mix by using the on/off pulse function until the ingredients are mostly blended. Continue mixing, gradually increasing the speed, until the mixture is smooth. Pour the smoothie into a glass and garnish with Berries on a Skewer (page 199), if desired.

Calories	179	Calcium	48 mg
Calories from fat	10	Iron	1 mg
Total fat	1 g	Potassium	506 mg
Carbohydrates	46 g	Beta Carotene	3133 mcg
Protein	2 g	Magnesium	17 mg
Fiber	6 g	Folic Acid	19 mcg

LOW-CAL SMOOTHIES

These cool drinks of fruit have 350 or fewer calories.

Shopping List

Fruit

Bananas

Blueberries

Cantaloupe

Cherries

Kiwifruit

Mangoes

Nectarines

Oranges

Papayas

Peaches

Pineapple

Raspberries

Strawberries

Juice and Nectar

Apricot nectar

Mango nectar

Orange juice

Peach nectar

Unsweetened mango juice

Unsweetened pineapple juice

White cranberry juice

Miscellaneous

Honey (optional)

Lemon sorbet

Mango sorbet

Orange sorbet

Raspberry sorbet

Strawberry sorbet

A Beautiful Rind

This prize-winning orange smoothie deserves its Ph.D. (perfectly healthy and delicious) status. Whether to enjoy it as a midday snack or as part of a meal is purely academic.

1 SERVING

½ cup orange juice

1 to 2 teaspoons honey (or to taste), optional

1 cup diced orange

½ cup diced banana

⅓ cup orange sorbet

Place all ingredients in a blender and mix by using the on/off pulse function until the ingredients are mostly blended. Continue mixing, gradually increasing the speed, until the mixture is smooth. Pour the smoothie into a glass and garnish the rim with an Orange Wheel (page 203), if desired.

Calories	303	Calcium	90 mg
Calories from fat	7	Iron	1 mg
Total fat	1 g	Potassium	924 mg
Carbohydrates	76 g	Beta Carotene	152 mcg
Protein	3 g	Magnesium	53 mg
Fiber	6 g	Folic Acid	106 mcg

Alicia Kiwis

If you're "In A Minor" funk, lift your spirits with this note-able smoothie made with kiwi, papaya, and banana.

1 SERVING

½ cup peach nectar

1 to 2 teaspoons honey (or to taste), optional

½ cup diced kiwi

½ cup diced papaya

½ cup diced banana

⅓ cup orange sorbet

Place all ingredients in a blender and mix by using the on/off pulse function until the ingredients are mostly blended. Continue mixing, gradually increasing the speed, until the mixture is smooth. Pour the smoothie into a glass and garnish with a Kumquat Lily (page 202), if desired.

Calories	340	Calcium	66 mg
Calories from fat	7	Iron	1 mg
Total fat	1 g	Potassium	694 mg
Carbohydrates	87 g	Beta Carotene	346 mcg
Protein	2 g	Magnesium	53 mg
Fiber	7 g	Folic Acid	49 mcg

Ba-Nanny Diaries

Find out what it's like to be spoiled by pampering yourself with this delicious, yet light smoothie from an otherwise obnoxiously rich family of drinks.

1 SERVING

½ cup mango nectar

1 to 2 teaspoons honey (or to taste), optional

1 cup diced pineapple

½ cup diced banana

⅓ cup lemon sorbet

Place all ingredients in a blender and mix by using the on/off pulse function until the ingredients are mostly blended. Continue mixing, gradually increasing the speed, until the mixture is smooth. Pour the smoothie into a glass and garnish with Mint Leaves (page 205), if desired.

Calories	298	Calcium	22 mg
Calories from fat	10	Iron	1 mg
Total fat	1 g	Potassium	563 mg
Carbohydrates	76 g	Beta Carotene	931 mcg
Protein	2 g	Magnesium	49 mg
Fiber	5 g	Folic Acid	35 mcg

Blue Velvet

This scrumptious blueberry smoothie is especially rich and satisfying. Sample this treat the next time you have friends over for a golden oldies party.

1 SERVING

½ cup mango nectar

1 to 2 teaspoons honey (or to taste), optional

1 cup blueberries

½ cup diced banana

⅓ cup orange sorbet

Place all ingredients in a blender and mix by using the on/off pulse function until the ingredients are mostly blended. Continue mixing, gradually increasing the speed, until the mixture is smooth. Pour the smoothie into a glass and garnish with Berries on a Skewer (page 199), if desired.

Calories	296	Calcium	51 mg
Calories from fat	13	Iron	1 mg
Total fat	2 g	Potassium	421 mg
Carbohydrates	78 g	Beta Carotene	912 mcg
Protein	2 g	Magnesium	27 mg
Fiber	9 g	Folic Acid	18 mcg

Cran Prix

Drink this high-performance cranberry, mango, banana, cherry, and sorbet smoothie in the morning and you'll be off to a racing start. For a special touch, serve along with a checkered-flag–inspired bowl of white and black raisins.

1 SERVING

½ cup white cranberry juice

1 to 2 teaspoons honey (or to taste), optional

½ cup diced mango

½ cup diced banana

½ cup diced cherries

⅓ cup mango sorbet

Place all ingredients in a blender and mix by using the on/off pulse function until the ingredients are mostly blended. Continue mixing, gradually increasing the speed, until the mixture is smooth. Pour the smoothie into a glass and garnish with a Pineapple Bow (page 207), if desired.

Calories	307	Calcium	24 mg
Calories from fat	12	Iron	1 mg
Total fat	1 g	Potassium	588 mg
Carbohydrates	77 g	Beta Carotene	2046 mcg
Protein	2 g	Magnesium	37 mg
Fiber	6 g	Folic Acid	29 mcg

Dole Lotta Shakin' Goin' On

Tell your friends to come on over, then bang away on those blender buttons and surprise them with ice-cold servings of this refreshing pineapple classic.

1 SERVING

½ cup apricot nectar

1 to 2 teaspoons honey (or to taste), optional

1 cup diced pineapple

½ cup raspberries

⅓ cup mango sorbet

Place all ingredients in a blender and mix by using the on/off pulse function until the ingredients are mostly blended. Continue mixing, gradually increasing the speed, until the mixture is smooth. Pour the smoothie into a glass and garnish the rim with a Star Fruit Slice (page 210), if desired.

Calories	255	Calcium	33 mg
Calories from fat	10	Iron	1 mg
Total fat	1 g	Potassium	412 mg
Carbohydrates	65 g	Beta Carotene	1030 mcg
Protein	2 g	Magnesium	39 mg
Fiber	7 g	Folic Acid	34 mcg

Durango Mango

Whether you've been riding the range or the subway, corral some friends after a busy day to share this delicately flavored smoothie.

1 SERVING

½ cup mango nectar

1 to 2 teaspoons honey (or to taste), optional

1 cup diced mango

½ cup blueberries

⅓ cup mango sorbet

Place all ingredients in a blender and mix by using the on/off pulse function until the ingredients are mostly blended. Continue mixing, gradually increasing the speed, until the mixture is smooth. Pour the smoothie into a glass and garnish with a Fruit Skewer (page 200), if desired.

Calories	288	Calcium	43 mg
Calories from fat	10	Iron	1 mg
Total fat	1 g	Potassium	328 mg
Carbohydrates	76 g	Beta Carotene	4728 mcg
Protein	2 g	Magnesium	20 mg
Fiber	8 g	Folic Acid	27 mcg

For Peach Sake

You don't have to give up everything good in life to stay trim. This richly flavored smoothie can be enjoyed guilt-free as a midday snack or energizing refresher.

1 SERVING

½ cup peach nectar

1 to 2 teaspoons honey (or to taste), optional

1 cup diced peach

½ cup diced banana

⅓ cup strawberry sorbet

Place all ingredients in a blender and mix by using the on/off pulse function until the ingredients are mostly blended. Continue mixing, gradually increasing the speed, until the mixture is smooth. Pour the smoothie into a glass and garnish the rim with a Strawberry Fan (page 211), if desired.

Calories	301	Calcium	19 mg
Calories from fat	5	Iron	1 mg
Total fat	1 g	Potassium	682 mg
Carbohydrates	76 g	Beta Carotene	645 mcg
Protein	2 g	Magnesium	39 mg
Fiber	7 g	Folic Acid	21 mcg

Genghis Cannes (A French Mango-lian Smoothie)

Plan to raid your refrigerator often for a glassful of this smoothie and see if you don't agree that it is the pièce de résistance *of refreshment.*

1 SERVING

½ cup unsweetened pineapple juice

1 to 2 teaspoons honey (or to taste), optional

½ cup diced mango

½ cup diced pineapple

½ cup diced banana

¼ cup mango sorbet

Place all ingredients in a blender by using the on/off pulse function until the ingredients are mostly blended. Continue mixing, gradually increasing the speed, until the mixture is smooth. Pour the smoothie into a glass and garnish the rim with a Pineapple Spear (page 208), if desired.

Calories	291	Calcium	39 mg
Calories from fat	9	Iron	1 mg
Total fat	1 g	Potassium	681 mg
Carbohydrates	74 g	Beta Carotene	1974 mcg
Protein	2 g	Magnesium	56 mg
Fiber	5 g	Folic Acid	63 mcg

Ice-Cool Sweethearts

When lemon sorbet, mango, and pineapple walk hand in hand, the end result is a smoothie that'll make you pucker up.

1 SERVING

½ cup mango nectar

1 to 2 teaspoons honey (or to taste), optional

1 cup diced mango

½ cup diced pineapple

⅓ cup lemon sorbet

Place all ingredients in a blender and mix by using the on/off pulse function until the ingredients are mostly blended. Continue mixing, gradually increasing the speed, until the mixture is smooth. Pour the smoothie into a glass and garnish the rim with an Orange, Lemon, and Cherry Combo (page 206), if desired.

Calories	301	Calcium	30 mg
Calories from fat	8	Iron	1 mg
Total fat	1 g	Potassium	416 mg
Carbohydrates	77 g	Beta Carotene	4737 mcg
Protein	1 g	Magnesium	31 mg
Fiber	5 g	Folic Acid	35 mcg

Lean Nectarine

This smoothie is a choice way to satisfy your craving for something sweet without adding unnecessary calories. Enjoy this cool drink as a refreshing post-workout treat.

1 SERVING

½ cup apricot nectar

1 to 2 teaspoons honey (or to taste), optional

1 cup diced nectarine

½ cup diced pineapple

⅓ cup orange sorbet

Place all ingredients in a blender and mix by using the on/off pulse function until the ingredients are mostly blended. Continue mixing, gradually increasing the speed, until the mixture is smooth. Pour the smoothie into a glass and garnish the rim with a Lime Wheel (page 203), if desired.

Calories	269	Calcium	21 mg
Calories from fat	10	Iron	1 mg
Total fat	1 g	Potassium	577 mg
Carbohydrates	68 g	Beta Carotene	1503 mcg
Protein	2 g	Magnesium	28 mg
Fiber	4 g	Folic Acid	15 mcg

Man-gooooooooooooal!

Ay caramba! *You'll get a real kick out of announcing to your family that you have whipped up a pitcherful of this best-in-the-World, Cup of mango sweetness. Make sure to have plenty of low-fat tortilla chips and salsa on hand.*

1 SERVING

½ cup unsweetened mango juice

1 to 2 teaspoons honey (or to taste), optional

1 cup diced mango

½ cup diced pineapple

½ cup mango sorbet

Place all ingredients in a blender and mix by using the on/off pulse function until the ingredients are mostly blended. Continue mixing, gradually increasing the speed, until the mixture is smooth. Pour the smoothie into a glass and garnish the rim with a Pineapple Wedge (page 208), if desired.

Calories	326	Calcium	72 mg
Calories from fat	7	Iron	1 mg
Total fat	1 g	Potassium	345 mg
Carbohydrates	84 g	Beta Carotene	3860 mcg
Protein	96 g	Magnesium	26 mg
Fiber	5 g	Folic Acid	32 mcg

Monday Night Fruitbowl

The next time you have friends over to root for your favorite football team, make extra points by calling a time-out and passing around glassfuls of this pineapple, orange, and banana smoothie. They'll get a real kick out of this powerhouse refreshment.

1 SERVING

½ cup apricot nectar

1 to 2 teaspoons honey (or to taste), optional

½ cup diced pineapple

½ cup diced orange

½ cup diced banana

⅓ cup orange sorbet

Place all ingredients in a blender and mix by using the on/off pulse function until the ingredients are mostly blended. Continue mixing, gradually increasing the speed, until the mixture is smooth. Pour the smoothie into a glass and garnish with a Kumquat Lily (page 202), if desired.

Calories	313	Calcium	55 mg
Calories from fat	8	Iron	1 mg
Total fat	1 g	Potassium	744 mg
Carbohydrates	80 g	Beta Carotene	1068 mcg
Protein	2 g	Magnesium	48 mg
Fiber	6 g	Folic Acid	51 mcg

My Cousin Skinny

Yo! You be the judge and tell me whether this isn't the best strawberry and mango smoothie you've ever tasted.

1 SERVING

½ cup peach nectar

1 to 2 teaspoons honey (or to taste), optional

1 cup diced strawberries

½ cup diced mango

⅓ cup orange sorbet

Place all ingredients in a blender and mix by using the on/off pulse function until the ingredients are mostly blended. Continue mixing, gradually increasing the speed, until the mixture is smooth. Pour the smoothie into a glass and garnish the rim with a Strawberry Fan (page 211), if desired.

Calories	260	Calcium	36 mg
Calories from fat	7	Iron	1 mg
Total fat	1 g	Potassium	484 mg
Carbohydrates	66 g	Beta Carotene	2107 mcg
Protein	2 g	Magnesium	28 mg
Fiber	6 g	Folic Acid	40 mcg

Raspberry Sor-Bet Watch

If you're concerned about flabby abs, this blueberry, orange, and banana smoothie will be a real lifesaver. It's great for a beach party.

1 SERVING

½ cup apricot nectar

1 to 2 teaspoons honey (or to taste), optional

½ cup blueberries

½ cup diced orange

½ cup diced banana

¼ cup raspberry sorbet

Place all ingredients in a blender and mix by using the on/off pulse function until the ingredients are mostly blended. Continue mixing, gradually increasing the speed, until the mixture is smooth. Pour the smoothie into a glass and garnish with Berries on a Skewer (page 199), if desired.

Calories	272	Calcium	69 mg
Calories from fat	10	Iron	1 mg
Total fat	1 g	Potassium	631 mg
Carbohydrates	70 g	Beta Carotene	1059 mcg
Protein	3 g	Magnesium	37 mg
Fiber	9 g	Folic Acid	43 mcg

Rocket Man-Go

When your stomach is growling and you think it's going to be a long, long time before your next real meal, grab an ice-cold glass of this mango, cantaloupe, and banana smoothie and drink it fast before there's any m-Elton.

1 SERVING

½ cup white cranberry juice

1 to 2 teaspoons honey (or to taste), optional

½ cup diced mango

½ cup diced cantaloupe

½ cup diced banana

¼ cup mango sorbet

Place all ingredients in a blender and mix by using the on/off pulse function until the ingredients are mostly blended. Continue mixing, gradually increasing the speed, until the mixture is smooth. Pour the smoothie into a glass and garnish with Melon Balls on a Skewer (page 204), if desired.

Calories	264	Calcium	21 mg
Calories from fat	7	Iron	1 mg
Total fat	1 g	Potassium	667 mg
Carbohydrates	67 g	Beta Carotene	3459 mcg
Protein	2 g	Magnesium	38 mg
Fiber	4 g	Folic Acid	39 mcg

Simple Simon the Papaya Man

Okay, so my lips got stuck together, but you get the idea. Simon says mix some mango and banana with papaya to see if this smoothie doesn't qualify as a perfect midday snack.

1 SERVING

½ cup mango nectar

1 to 2 teaspoons honey (or to taste), optional

1 cup diced papaya

½ cup diced banana

⅓ cup mango sorbet

Place all ingredients in a blender and mix by using the on/off pulse function until the ingredients are mostly blended. Continue mixing, gradually increasing the speed, until the mixture is smooth. Pour the smoothie into a glass and garnish the rim with an Orange, Lemon, and Cherry Combo (page 206), if desired.

Calories	277	Calcium	44 mg
Calories from fat	6	Iron	0 mg
Total fat	1 g	Potassium	727 mg
Carbohydrates	71 g	Beta Carotene	982 mcg
Protein	2 g	Magnesium	41 mg
Fiber	6 g	Folic Acid	71 mcg

Tang Top

There are lots of ways to stay cool in the summer, but this orange-flavored fruit refresher is one of the best. Enjoy this low-cal offering with an assortment of sliced fruit.

1 SERVING

½ cup peach nectar

1 to 2 teaspoons honey (or to taste), optional

1 cup diced orange

½ cup diced pineapple

⅓ cup orange sorbet

Place all ingredients in a blender and mix by using the on/off pulse function until the ingredients are mostly blended. Continue mixing, gradually increasing the speed, until the mixture is smooth. Pour the smoothie into a glass and garnish the rim with an Orange Wheel (page 203), if desired.

Calories	283	Calcium	84 mg
Calories from fat	5	Iron	1 mg
Total fat	1 g	Potassium	517 mg
Carbohydrates	72 g	Beta Carotene	236 mcg
Protein	2 g	Magnesium	34 mg
Fiber	6 g	Folic Acid	64 mcg

Today You Are a Mango

Mazel tov! Don't let it be another 13 years before your next glass of this sensational mango, kiwi, and banana smoothie. By then, you'll be a doctor.

1 SERVING

½ cup unsweetened mango juice

1 to 2 teaspoons honey (or to taste), optional

½ cup diced mango

½ cup diced kiwi

½ cup diced banana

⅓ cup mango sorbet

Place all ingredients in a blender and mix by using the on/off pulse function until the ingredients are mostly blended. Continue mixing, gradually increasing the speed, until the mixture is smooth. Pour the smoothie into a glass and garnish the rim with a Star Fruit Slice (page 210), if desired.

Calories	317	Calcium	86 mg
Calories from fat	9	Iron	1 mg
Total fat	1 g	Potassium	720 mg
Carbohydrates	80 g	Beta Carotene	2057 mcg
Protein	97 g	Magnesium	56 mg
Fiber	7 g	Folic Acid	59 mcg

Tropical Twister

You may get carried away by the Caribbean flavors of this enticing smoothie. Invite friends over for a pool party and serve up glassfuls of this tropical delight accompanied by slices of low-calorie banana bread.

1 SERVING

½ cup orange juice

1 to 2 teaspoons honey (or to taste), optional

½ cup diced pineapple

½ cup diced mango

½ cup diced banana

¼ cup mango sorbet

Place all ingredients in a blender and mix by using the on/off pulse function until the ingredients are mostly blended. Continue mixing, gradually increasing the speed, until the mixture is smooth. Pour the smoothie into a glass and garnish the rim with a Pineapple Slice (page 208), if desired.

Calories	276	Calcium	32 mg
Calories from fat	10	Iron	1 mg
Total fat	1 g	Potassium	761 mg
Carbohydrates	70 g	Beta Carotene	2017 mcg
Protein	2 g	Magnesium	54 mg
Fiber	5 g	Folic Acid	72 mcg

Uptown Whirl

This classy mango smoothie is rich in flavor yet surprisingly low in calories. It's the perfect treat after a workout at the club.

1 SERVING

½ cup mango nectar

1 to 2 teaspoons honey (or to taste), optional

1 cup diced mango

½ cup diced banana

¼ cup orange sorbet

Place all ingredients in a blender and mix by using the on/off pulse function until the ingredients are mostly blended. Continue mixing, gradually increasing the speed, until the mixture is smooth. Pour the smoothie into a glass and garnish the rim with an Orange Wheel (page 203), if desired.

Calories	319	Calcium	27 mg
Calories from fat	8	Iron	1 mg
Total fat	1 g	Potassium	665 mg
Carbohydrates	83 g	Beta Carotene	4764 mcg
Protein	2 g	Magnesium	42 mg
Fiber	6 g	Folic Acid	41 mcg

You Make Me Peel So Young

Ol' Blue Eyes couldn't have said it better. This zest-fully flavored orange and pineapple smoothie promises to put a spring in your step. Have a glass-ful before heading for the gym and you'll be one happy individual.

1 SERVING

½ cup apricot nectar

1 to 2 teaspoons honey (or to taste), optional

1 cup diced orange

½ cup diced pineapple

⅓ cup orange sorbet

Place all ingredients in a blender and mix by using the on/off pulse function until the ingredients are mostly blended. Continue mixing, gradually increasing the speed, until the mixture is smooth. Pour the smoothie into a glass and garnish with Mint Leaves (page 205), if desired.

Calories	286	Calcium	86 mg
Calories from fat	6	Iron	1 mg
Total fat	1 g	Potassium	610 mg
Carbohydrates	73 g	Beta Carotene	1067 mcg
Protein	2 g	Magnesium	35 mg
Fiber	6 g	Folic Acid	64 mcg

CHAPTER 5

Smoothie Digni-Dairies

For many of us, being on a diet implies giving up al! the foods we enjoy most. Included in this list of forbidden foods are all the decadently rich, creamy, and high-calorie beverages that taste so good. While a simple smoothie of fruit and fruit juice always refreshes and satisfies, when you're craving something richer, treat yourself to a smoothie made with dairy products. They not only endow a smoothie with a creamier texture and more intense flavor, but, just as important, this combination of ingredients also allows you to reap the health benefits of both fruit and dairy—vital components of the food pyramid. Once you have enjoyed the smooth-as-silk taste of such creations as Slenderella (page 102) or Rasp-ody in Blue (page

126), you'll be eager to sample all 44 smoothie recipes in this chapter.

As you read through these recipes, you will note that most of them call for lowfat or nonfat ingredients. However, if you are not watching your calorie intake, feel free to substitute regular yogurt or ice cream, if that suits your taste. On the other hand, if you are seeking more ways to add soybean products to your diet, try substituting tofu, soy milk, and soy yogurt for the dairy products included in these recipes.

It doesn't matter if you're dieting—the fruit in these smoothies is temptingly fresh, and your favorite dairy products are rich and creamy. So head for the blender and whip up one of the most satisfying, low-cal taste treats imaginable. You'll be moooooooost happy you did!

SUPER LOW-CAL SMOOTHIES

These luscious smoothies have 250 or fewer calories.

Shopping List

Fruit

Apricots	Oranges
Bananas	Peaches
Blueberries	Pineapple
Cantaloupe	Raspberries
Cherries	Strawberries
Kiwifruit	Tangerines (or
Mangos	clementines)

Juice and Nectar

Mango nectar
Orange juice
Unsweetened apple
    juice
Unsweetened guava
    juice
Unsweetened mango
    juice
Unsweetened peach
    juice
Unsweetened pine-
    apple juice
White cranberry juice

Miscellaneous

Lowfat banana frozen
    yogurt
Lowfat blueberry
    frozen yogurt
Lowfat cherry frozen
    yogurt
Lowfat milk
    (2 percent)
Lowfat strawberry
    frozen yogurt
Honey (optional)
Nonfat blueberry
    yogurt
Nonfat lime yogurt
Nonfat raspberry
    yogurt
Nonfat strawberry
    yogurt
Nonfat vanilla frozen
    yogurt
Nonfat vanilla yogurt
Vanilla extract

Berry Slender

This berry rich smoothie will banish any craving you may have for something rich and sinful—and you'll be berry happy to know you can indulge in this guilt-free smoothie any time of the day.

1 SERVING

½ cup unsweetened pineapple juice

1 to 2 teaspoons honey (or to taste), optional

½ cup raspberries

½ cup blueberries

½ cup diced strawberries

¼ cup nonfat vanilla yogurt

Place all ingredients in a blender and mix by using the on/off pulse function until the ingredients are mostly blended. Continue mixing, gradually increasing the speed, until the mixture is smooth. Pour the smoothie into a glass and garnish with Berries on a Skewer (page 199), if desired.

Calories	209	Calcium	174 mg
Calories from fat	12	Iron	1 mg
Total fat	1 g	Potassium	527 mg
Carbohydrates	49 g	Beta Carotene	40 mcg
Protein	5 g	Magnesium	45 mg
Fiber	9 g	Folic Acid	65 mcg

Better Lite Than Never

You don't want to regret missing an opportunity to taste this light and refreshing mango, pineapple, and raspberry smoothie. Whether enjoyed as part of your morning fare, or even as an after-dinner snack, it's never too late.

1 SERVING

½ cup orange juice

1 to 2 teaspoons honey (or to taste), optional

½ cup diced mango

½ cup diced pineapple

½ cup raspberries

½ cup nonfat raspberry yogurt

Place all ingredients in a blender and mix by using the on/off pulse function until the ingredients are mostly blended. Continue mixing, gradually increasing the speed, until the mixture is smooth. Pour the smoothie into a glass and garnish the rim with a Pineapple Slice (page 208), if desired.

Calories	237	Calcium	216 mg
Calories from fat	10	Iron	1 mg
Total fat	1 g	Potassium	743 mg
Carbohydrates	55 g	Beta Carotene	2005 mcg
Protein	6 g	Magnesium	43 mg
Fiber	7 g	Folic Acid	73 mcg

Bing in 'Da Noise

If you're looking for an energizing treat, then tap on over to your blender and whip up this award-winning cherry and banana smoothie. It's funky, it's delicious, and it's certain to bring you rave reviews.

1 SERVING

½ cup unsweetened guava juice

1 to 2 teaspoons honey (or to taste), optional

½ cup diced cherries

½ cup diced banana

¼ cup lowfat cherry or nonfat vanilla frozen yogurt

Place all ingredients in a blender and mix by using the on/off pulse function until the ingredients are mostly blended. Continue mixing, gradually increasing the speed, until the mixture is smooth. Pour the smoothie into a glass and garnish with a Pineapple Bow (page 207), if desired.

Calories	232	Calcium	102 mg
Calories from fat	15	Iron	1 mg
Total fat	2 g	Potassium	558 mg
Carbohydrates	53 g	Beta Carotene	120 mcg
Protein	4 g	Magnesium	37 mg
Fiber	31 g	Folic Acid	22 mcg

Chico and the Mango

Fusing mango, orange, and banana together may seem like an odd combination, but this smoothie tastes fabulous. Reward yourself with a glassful when you get home from the gym.

1 SERVING

½ cup unsweetened mango juice

1 to 2 teaspoons honey (or to taste), optional

½ cup diced mango

½ cup diced orange

½ cup diced banana

¼ cup nonfat lime yogurt

Place all ingredients in a blender and mix by using the on/off pulse function until the ingredients are mostly blended. Continue mixing, gradually increasing the speed, until the mixture is smooth. Pour the smoothie into a glass and garnish the rim with a Lime Wheel (page 203), if desired.

Calories	250	Calcium	149 mg
Calories from fat	6	Iron	1 mg
Total fat	1 g	Potassium	664 mg
Carbohydrates	63 g	Beta Carotene	1997 mcg
Protein	99 g	Magnesium	38 mg
Fiber	6 g	Folic Acid	53 mcg

Doonesberry

Commune with Mike, Joanie, Mark, and the rest of the gang as you enjoy this fantastic raspberry and banana smoothie. It's the perfect chilled refreshment to enjoy after tennis or a brisk jog.

1 SERVING

½ cup orange juice

1 to 2 teaspoons honey (or to taste), optional

1 cup diced banana

½ cup raspberries

¼ cup nonfat raspberry yogurt

Place all ingredients in a blender and mix by using the on/off pulse function until the ingredients are mostly blended. Continue mixing, gradually increasing the speed, until the mixture is smooth. Pour the smoothie into a glass and garnish with Berries on a Skewer (page 199), if desired.

Calories	250	Calcium	124 mg
Calories from fat	12	Iron	1 mg
Total fat	1 g	Potassium	1028 mg
Carbohydrates	61 g	Beta Carotene	142 mcg
Protein	5 g	Magnesium	68 mg
Fiber	8 g	Folic Acid	82 mcg

Fill 'Er Up Twister

This smoothie will fill you up but not out! So if great taste and satisfaction is what you're after, pull up to the nearest blender and whip up a batch of this high-octane, low-calorie strawberry and peach smoothie. Get even more mileage by serving it with an assortment of lowfat strawberry filled cookies.

1 SERVING

½ cup unsweetened peach juice

1 to 2 teaspoons honey (or to taste), optional

½ cup diced strawberries

½ cup diced peach

½ cup diced banana

¼ cup nonfat strawberry yogurt

Place all ingredients in a blender and mix by using the on/off pulse function until the ingredients are mostly blended. Continue mixing, gradually increasing the speed, until the mixture is smooth. Pour the smoothie into a glass and garnish the rim with a Strawberry Fan (page 211), if desired.

Calories	218	Calcium	107 mg
Calories from fat	6	Iron	1 mg
Total fat	1 g	Potassium	686 mg
Carbohydrates	53 g	Beta Carotene	274 mcg
Protein	4 g	Magnesium	35 mg
Fiber	5 g	Folic Acid	30 mcg

Have a Berry Merry Christmas

Why serve eggnog when you can indulge in this festive strawberry, banana, and blueberry smoothie instead? You'll welcome this ultra-low-calorie treat any time of the year.

1 SERVING

½ cup unsweetened apple juice

1 to 2 teaspoons honey (or to taste), optional

½ cup diced strawberries

½ cup blueberries

½ cup diced banana

¼ cup nonfat vanilla yogurt

Place all ingredients in a blender and mix by using the on/off pulse function until the ingredients are mostly blended. Continue mixing, gradually increasing the speed, until the mixture is smooth. Pour the smoothie into a glass and garnish with an Apple Chip (page 195), if desired.

Calories	236	Calcium	153 mg
Calories from fat	12	Iron	1 mg
Total fat	1 g	Potassium	710 mg
Carbohydrates	57 g	Beta Carotene	49 mcg
Protein	5 g	Magnesium	44 mg
Fiber	7 g	Folic Acid	35 mcg

Hawaiian De-Lite

This delightful pineapple-flavored smoothie is a definite crowd pleaser. Whip up batches of it to serve to friends as you lounge around the pool.

1 SERVING

½ cup unsweetened pineapple juice

1 to 2 teaspoons honey (or to taste), optional

¾ cup diced pineapple

½ cup diced banana

¼ cup nonfat vanilla yogurt

Place all ingredients in a blender and mix by using the on/off pulse function until the ingredients are mostly blended. Continue mixing, gradually increasing the speed, until the mixture is smooth. Pour the smoothie into a glass and garnish the rim with a Star Fruit Slice (page 210), if desired.

Calories	250	Calcium	143 mg
Calories from fat	10	Iron	1 mg
Total fat	1 g	Potassium	736 mg
Carbohydrates	60 g	Beta Carotene	53 mcg
Protein	2 g	Magnesium	65 mg
Fiber	3 g	Folic Acid	62 mcg

Hic-Kiwi Dic-Kiwi Dock

You don't have to wait for the clock to strike one to enjoy this delightful kiwi, banana, and peach smoothie. It's so low in calories, you can drink it any time of the day.

1 SERVING

½ cup mango nectar

1 to 2 teaspoons honey (or to taste), optional

½ cup diced kiwi

¼ cup diced banana

½ cup diced peach

¼ cup lowfat banana or nonfat vanilla frozen yogurt

Place all ingredients in a blender and mix by using the on/off pulse function until the ingredients are mostly blended. Continue mixing, gradually increasing the speed, until the mixture is smooth. Pour the smoothie into a glass and garnish with a Kumquat Lily (page 202), if desired.

Calories	248	Calcium	112 mg
Calories from fat	13	Iron	1 mg
Total fat	1 g	Potassium	779 mg
Carbohydrates	60 g	Beta Carotene	1216 mcg
Protein	4 g	Magnesium	56 mg
Fiber	7 g	Folic Acid	52 mcg

Love Me Slender

The word on the street is that the King himself has been spotted at a supermarket, a mall, and a drugstore enjoying a glass of this low-calorie fruit and yogurt smoothie. Invite friends over to Grace your Land and enjoy a night of nostalgia, featuring golden oldies and glassfuls of this rocking-good smoothie.

1 SERVING

½ cup unsweetened pineapple juice

1 to 2 teaspoons honey (or to taste), optional

½ cup blueberries

½ cup diced cherries

½ cup diced banana

¼ cup nonfat strawberry yogurt

Place all ingredients in a blender and mix by using the on/off pulse function until the ingredients are mostly blended. Continue mixing, gradually increasing the speed, until the mixture is smooth. Pour the smoothie into a glass and garnish the rim with a Strawberry Fan (page 211), if desired.

Calories	250	Calcium	144 mg
Calories from fat	15	Iron	1 mg
Total fat	2 g	Potassium	722 mg
Carbohydrates	61 g	Beta Carotene	124 mcg
Protein	5 g	Magnesium	46 mg
Fiber	7 g	Folic Acid	46 mcg

Mel-on Wheels

Start the morning with a glassful of this fuel-packed cantaloupe, apricot, and mango smoothie and see how it accelerates you into the fast lane for the rest of the day.

1 SERVING

½ cup orange juice

1 to 2 teaspoons honey (or to taste), optional

½ cup diced cantaloupe

½ cup diced apricots

½ cup diced mango

¼ cup nonfat lime yogurt

Place all ingredients in a blender and mix by using the on/off pulse function until the ingredients are mostly blended. Continue mixing, gradually increasing the speed, until the mixture is smooth. Pour the smoothie into a glass and garnish the rim with a Lime Wheel (page 203), if desired.

Calories	204	Calcium	91 mg
Calories from fat	9	Iron	1 mg
Total fat	1 g	Potassium	922 mg
Carbohydrates	48 g	Beta Carotene	4676 mcg
Protein	5 g	Magnesium	36 mg
Fiber	4 g	Folic Acid	69 mcg

NYPD Blueberries

It would be a crime not to try this blueberry smoothie, which is low in calories yet dramatically rich in flavor. Serve it when your family is gathered in front of the television.

1 SERVING

½ cup orange juice

1 to 2 teaspoons honey (or to taste), optional

½ cup blueberries

½ cup diced mango

½ cup diced strawberries

¼ cup lowfat blueberry or nonfat vanilla frozen
   yogurt

Place all ingredients in a blender and mix by using the on/off pulse function until the ingredients are mostly blended. Continue mixing, gradually increasing the speed, until the mixture is smooth. Pour the smoothie into a glass and garnish with Berries on a Skewer (page 199), if desired.

Calories	213	Calcium	129 mg
Calories from fat	17	Iron	1 mg
Total fat	2 g	Potassium	601 mg
Carbohydrates	50 g	Beta Carotene	1984 mcg
Protein	4 g	Magnesium	36 mg
Fiber	6 g	Folic Acid	67 mcg

Po-kiwi-mon

There may be 250 creatures found in the Pokemon universe, but all you need to make this simple smoothie is some kiwi, banana, and pineapple. It must be the magical power of its name that allows this cool creation to taste so good, yet be amazingly low in calories and fat.

1 SERVING

½ cup unsweetened pineapple juice

1 to 2 teaspoons honey (or to taste), optional

½ cup diced kiwi

½ cup diced pineapple

½ cup diced banana

¼ cup nonfat lime yogurt

Place all ingredients in a blender and mix by using the on/off pulse function until the ingredients are mostly blended. Continue mixing, gradually increasing the speed, until the mixture is smooth. Pour the smoothie into a glass and garnish with a Banana Wafer (page 197), if desired.

Calories	250	Calcium	104 mg
Calories from fat	11	Iron	1 mg
Total fat	1 g	Potassium	921 mg
Carbohydrates	63 g	Beta Carotene	144 mcg
Protein	4 g	Magnesium	75 mg
Fiber	6 g	Folic Acid	85 mcg

Practice What You Peach

Set a good example for your family by serving them this refreshing, healthful, low-cal smoothie brimming with the rich flavors of peach and banana.

1 SERVING

½ cup unsweetened peach juice

1 to 2 teaspoons honey (or to taste), optional

1 cup diced peach

½ cup diced banana

¼ cup nonfat vanilla frozen yogurt

Place all ingredients in a blender and mix by using the on/off pulse function until the ingredients are mostly blended. Continue mixing, gradually increasing the speed, until the mixture is smooth. Pour the smoothie into a glass and garnish with Mint Leaves (page 205), if desired.

Calories	250	Calcium	111 mg
Calories from fat	5	Iron	1 mg
Total fat	1 g	Potassium	758 mg
Carbohydrates	63 g	Beta Carotene	488 mcg
Protein	5 g	Magnesium	43 mg
Fiber	5 g	Folic Acid	25 mcg

Skim Specialist

A second opinion won't be necessary. The cure for those extra pounds is to eat a balance of healthful foods, including this strawberry, blueberry, and banana smoothie. It's just what the doctor ordered.

1 SERVING

¼ cup lowfat (2 percent) milk

¼ cup white cranberry juice

1 to 2 teaspoons honey (or to taste), optional

½ cup diced strawberries

½ cup blueberries

½ cup diced banana

¼ cup nonfat blueberry yogurt

Place all ingredients in a blender and mix by using the on/off pulse function until the ingredients are mostly blended. Continue mixing, gradually increasing the speed, until the mixture is smooth. Pour the smoothie into a glass and garnish the rim with a Strawberry Fan (page 211), if desired.

Calories	211	Calcium	190 mg
Calories from fat	22	Iron	1 mg
Total fat	2 g	Potassium	616 mg
Carbohydrates	47 g	Beta Carotene	48 mcg
Protein	6 g	Magnesium	29 mg
Fiber	7 g	Folic Acid	28 mcg

Slenderella

Don't wait for your fairy godmother to serve you this ultra-low-cal smoothie. Just become a glass sipper (and be certain to take your last gulp before the clock strikes midnight).

1 SERVING

½ cup orange juice

1 to 2 teaspoons honey (or to taste), optional

½ cup diced peach

½ cup diced banana

½ cup raspberries

¼ cup nonfat raspberry yogurt

Place all ingredients in a blender and mix by using the on/off pulse function until the ingredients are mostly blended. Continue mixing, gradually increasing the speed, until the mixture is smooth. Pour the smoothie into a glass and garnish with Berries on a Skewer (page 199), if desired.

Calories	221	Calcium	123 mg
Calories from fat	9	Iron	1 mg
Total fat	1 g	Potassium	898 mg
Carbohydrates	53 g	Beta Carotene	332 mcg
Protein	5 g	Magnesium	52 mg
Fiber	8 g	Folic Acid	70 mcg

The Cold Spin Zone

No matter how you spin the cantaloupe, banana, and yogurt together, you still come up with an honest-to-goodness delicious smoothie. Explain to your friends that this delectable treat has fewer than 250 calories, and watch for the "oh really" factor in their amazed reaction.

1 SERVING

½ cup orange juice

1 to 2 teaspoons honey (or to taste), optional

1 cup diced cantaloupe

½ cup diced banana

¼ cup nonfat vanilla yogurt

Place all ingredients in a blender and mix by using the on/off pulse function until the ingredients are mostly blended. Continue mixing, gradually increasing the speed, until the mixture is smooth. Pour the smoothie into a glass and garnish with Melon Balls on a Skewer (page 204), if desired.

Calories	235	Calcium	144 mg
Calories from fat	10	Iron	1 mg
Total fat	1 g	Potassium	1167 mg
Carbohydrates	54 g	Beta Carotene	3077 mcg
Protein	6 g	Magnesium	63 mg
Fiber	3 g	Folic Acid	85 mcg

The Lite at the End of the Funnel

When you feel overwhelmed by life's daily challenges, take a break and indulge in a glassful of this light and delicious strawberry and cantaloupe concoction.

1 SERVING

½ cup unsweetened apple juice

1 to 2 teaspoons honey (or to taste), optional

1 cup diced strawberries

½ cup diced cantaloupe

¼ cup lowfat strawberry or nonfat vanilla frozen yogurt

Place all ingredients in a blender and mix by using the on/off pulse function until the ingredients are mostly blended. Continue mixing, gradually increasing the speed, until the mixture is smooth. Pour the smoothie into a glass and garnish with an Apple Chip (page 195), if desired.

Calories	182	Calcium	115 mg
Calories from fat	14	Iron	1 mg
Total fat	2 g	Potassium	739 mg
Carbohydrates	41 g	Beta Carotene	1523 mcg
Protein	4 g	Magnesium	35 mg
Fiber	4 g	Folic Acid	45 mcg

Thin Sync

There are "No Strings Attached" when I say that this cherry, mango, and banana smoothie will achieve "Celebrity" status in your home. This star-studded smoothie is so low in fat and calories, you can sample it without guilt any time of the day.

1 SERVING

½ cup orange juice

1 to 2 teaspoons honey (or to taste), optional

½ cup diced cherries

½ cup diced mango

½ cup blueberries

¼ cup nonfat raspberry yogurt

Place all ingredients in a blender and mix by using the on/off pulse function until the ingredients are mostly blended. Continue mixing, gradually increasing the speed, until the mixture is smooth. Pour the smoothie into a glass and garnish with a Kumquat Lily (page 202), if desired.

Calories	222	Calcium	140 mg
Calories from fat	15	Iron	1 mg
Total fat	2 g	Potassium	632 mg
Carbohydrates	53 g	Beta Carotene	2056 mcg
Protein	5 g	Magnesium	29 mg
Fiber	6 g	Folic Acid	52 mcg

Tiny Trim

There's still hope for that size 6 dress or those trousers with the 32-inch waist. Include this scrumptious kiwi, strawberry, banana, and yogurt smoothie in your diet plan, and watch the pounds disappear.

1 SERVING

½ cup unsweetened apple juice

1 to 2 teaspoons honey (or to taste), optional

½ cup diced kiwi

½ cup diced strawberries

½ cup diced banana

¼ cup nonfat strawberry yogurt

Place all ingredients in a blender and mix by using the on/off pulse function until the ingredients are mostly blended. Continue mixing, gradually increasing the speed, until the mixture is smooth. Pour the smoothie into a glass and garnish the rim with a Strawberry Fan (page 211), if desired.

Calories	234	Calcium	134 mg
Calories from fat	11	Iron	1 mg
Total fat	1 g	Potassium	959 mg
Carbohydrates	56 g	Beta Carotene	144 mcg
Protein	4 g	Magnesium	60 mg
Fiber	7 g	Folic Acid	62 mcg

To Diet For

When you're trying to lose weight, rev up a glassful of this tangy smoothie enriched with pineapple, peach, yogurt, and those darling clementines, and you'll enjoy instant satisfaction in a glass.

1 SERVING

½ cup unsweetened apple juice

1 to 2 teaspoons honey (or to taste), optional

⅛ teaspoon vanilla extract

½ cup diced tangerine (or clementine),
   seeds removed

½ cup diced peach

½ cup diced pineapple

¼ cup nonfat vanilla frozen yogurt

Place all ingredients in a blender and mix by using the on/off pulse function until the ingredients are mostly blended. Continue mixing, gradually increasing the speed, until the mixture is smooth. Pour the smoothie into a glass and garnish the rim with a Pineapple Wedge (page 208), if desired.

Calories	250	Calcium	132 mg
Calories from fat	5	Iron	1 mg
Total fat	1 g	Potassium	744 mg
Carbohydrates	62 g	Beta Carotene	768 mcg
Protein	4 g	Magnesium	46 mg
Fiber	4 g	Folic Acid	56 mcg

LOW-CAL SMOOTHIES

These smoothies contain 350 or fewer calories.

Shopping List

Fruit

Apples
Apricots
Bananas
Blueberries
Cantaloupe
Cherries
Kiwifruit
Mangos

Nectarines
Oranges
Peaches
Pears
Pineapple
Raspberries
Strawberries

Juice and Nectar

Apple cider
Apricot nectar
Orange juice
Peach nectar
Pear nectar
Unsweetened apple
   juice

Unsweetened guava
   juice
Unsweetened peach
   juice
Honey (optional)
Unsweetened pine-
   apple juice
White cranberry juice

Miscellaneous

Honey (optional)
Lowfat banana frozen
   yogurt
Lowfat blueberry
   frozen yogurt
Lowfat blueberry yogurt
Lowfat cherry frozen
   yogurt
Lowfat milk (2 percent)
Lowfat peach frozen
   yogurt

Lowfat pineapple
   frozen yogurt
Lowfat raspberry
   frozen yogurt
Lowfat strawberry
   frozen yogurt
Nonfat vanilla frozen
   yogurt
Nonfat vanilla yogurt
Vanilla extract

Ally McPeel

You can't lose a thing (except pounds) with this calorie-reduced apple sensation. It's definitely a thin-thin situation. Enjoy a glassful before heading out to the gym.

1 SERVING

½ cup pear nectar

1 to 2 teaspoons honey (or to taste), optional

1 cup diced apple

½ cup diced banana

⅓ cup lowfat banana or nonfat vanilla frozen yogurt

Place all ingredients in a blender and mix by using the on/off pulse function until the ingredients are mostly blended. Continue mixing, gradually increasing the speed, until the mixture is smooth. Pour the smoothie into a glass and garnish with an Apple Chip (page 195), if desired.

Calories	277	Calcium	121 mg
Calories from fat	15	Iron	1 mg
Total fat	2 g	Potassium	571 mg
Carbohydrates	66 g	Beta Carotene	59 mcg
Protein	4 g	Magnesium	41 mg
Fiber	6 g	Folic Acid	25 mcg

Banana and the King

The wonderful flavors of banana, orange, and mango govern the taste of this epic smoothie. Siam not kidding when I say this is the king of all smoothies. Thai it!

1 SERVING

½ cup orange juice

1 to 2 teaspoons honey (or to taste), optional

½ cup diced banana

½ cup diced orange

½ cup diced mango

¼ cup lowfat banana or nonfat vanilla frozen
   yogurt

Place all ingredients in a blender and mix by using the on/off pulse function until the ingredients are mostly blended. Continue mixing, gradually increasing the speed, until the mixture is smooth. Pour the smoothie into a glass and garnish with a Banana Wafer (page 197), if desired.

Calories	272	Calcium	139 mg
Calories from fat	14	Iron	1 mg
Total fat	2 g	Potassium	935 mg
Carbohydrates	64 g	Beta Carotene	2043 mcg
Protein	5 g	Magnesium	59 mg
Fiber	6 g	Folic Acid	95 mcg

Bing It On!

If a cherry smoothie could win a national title for originality and great taste, this is it. Serve this Number one winner to friends or family while cheering on your favorite team.

1 SERVING

½ cup apricot nectar

1 to 2 teaspoons honey (or to taste), optional

½ cup diced cherries

½ cup diced banana

½ cup diced mango

¼ cup lowfat cherry or nonfat vanilla frozen yogurt

Place all ingredients in a blender and mix by using the on/off pulse function until the ingredients are mostly blended. Continue mixing, gradually increasing the speed, until the mixture is smooth. Pour the smoothie into a glass and garnish with a Pineapple Bow (page 207), if desired.

Calories	296	Calcium	109 mg
Calories from fat	18	Iron	1 mg
Total fat	2 g	Potassium	829 mg
Carbohydrates	71 g	Beta Carotene	3033 mcg
Protein	5 g	Magnesium	51 mg
Fiber	6 g	Folic Acid	35 mcg

Blue Lite Special

Attention, smoothie lovers! If you've been shopping around for an outstandingly rich blueberry smoothie that's had its calories slashed, then this one is for you. Such a deal!

1 SERVING

⅓ cup unsweetened guava juice

1 to 2 teaspoons honey (or to taste), optional

1 cup blueberries

½ cup diced cherries

½ cup lowfat blueberry or nonfat vanilla frozen yogurt

Place all ingredients in a blender and mix by using the on/off pulse function until the ingredients are mostly blended. Continue mixing, gradually increasing the speed, until the mixture is smooth. Pour the smoothie into a glass and garnish with Berries on a Skewer (page 199), if desired.

Calories	254	Calcium	211 mg
Calories from fat	27	Iron	1 mg
Total fat	3 g	Potassium	359 mg
Carbohydrates	57 g	Beta Carotene	84 mcg
Protein	6 g	Magnesium	23 mg
Fiber	8 g	Folic Acid	12 mcg

Cherry-ots of Fire

If winning the diet game is important to you, try this delicious cherry-flavored smoothie that has an excellent track record. It's especially refreshing after a long jog on a hot afternoon.

1 SERVING

½ cup unsweetened apple juice

1 to 2 teaspoons honey (or to taste), optional

1 cup diced cherries

½ cup diced banana

¼ cup lowfat cherry or nonfat vanilla frozen yogurt

Place all ingredients in a blender and mix by using the on/off pulse function until the ingredients are mostly blended. Continue mixing, gradually increasing the speed, until the mixture is smooth. Pour the smoothie into a glass and garnish the rim with an Orange, Lemon, and Cherry Combo (page 206), if desired.

Calories	283	Calcium	112 mg
Calories from fat	23	Iron	1 mg
Total fat	3 g	Potassium	868 mg
Carbohydrates	65 g	Beta Carotene	205 mcg
Protein	5 g	Magnesium	49 mg
Fiber	5 g	Folic Acid	25 mcg

Cider Man

This cider-enriched smoothie will give you the power to ward off those evil hunger pangs. Try it, and it will be just a matter of time until you can fit into those tights.

1 SERVING

½ cup apple cider

1 to 2 teaspoons honey (or to taste), optional

½ cup diced pineapple

½ cup diced cantaloupe

½ cup diced banana

¼ cup lowfat pineapple or nonfat vanilla frozen yogurt

Place all ingredients in a blender and mix by using the on/off pulse function until the ingredients are mostly blended. Continue mixing, gradually increasing the speed, until the mixture is smooth. Pour the smoothie into a glass and garnish with an Apple Chip (page 195), if desired.

Calories	251	Calcium	95 mg
Calories from fat	14	Iron	1 mg
Total fat	2 g	Potassium	724 mg
Carbohydrates	58 g	Beta Carotene	1543 mcg
Protein	4 g	Magnesium	49 mg
Fiber	3 g	Folic Acid	41 mcg

Good Lite, Moon

If you're looking for just the right smoothie to enjoy at the end of the day, first say good night to the potato chips, candy bar, and cookies, and indulge instead in this low-calorie smoothie.

1 SERVING

½ cup peach nectar

1 to 2 teaspoons honey (or to taste), optional

½ cup diced peach

½ cup diced cherries

½ cup diced banana

⅓ cup lowfat peach or nonfat vanilla frozen yogurt

Place all ingredients in a blender and mix by using the on/off pulse function until the ingredients are mostly blended. Continue mixing, gradually increasing the speed, until the mixture is smooth. Pour the smoothie into a glass and garnish the rim with a Star Fruit Slice (page 210), if desired.

Calories	293	Calcium	128 mg
Calories from fat	18	Iron	1 mg
Total fat	2 g	Potassium	808 mg
Carbohydrates	69 g	Beta Carotene	503 mcg
Protein	6 g	Magnesium	50 mg
Fiber	6 g	Folic Acid	27 mcg

It's All Lite with Me

It's never the wrong time to be tempted by a glass-ful of this peach and raspberry smoothie. It's so low in calories—yet bursting with intense flavors—that you won't be able to resist it.

1 SERVING

½ cup apricot nectar

1 to 2 teaspoons honey (or to taste), optional

1 cup diced peach

½ cup raspberries

½ cup lowfat raspberry or nonfat vanilla frozen yogurt

Place all ingredients in a blender and mix by using the on/off pulse function until the ingredients are mostly blended. Continue mixing, gradually increasing the speed, until the mixture is smooth. Pour the smoothie into a glass and garnish with Berries on a Skewer (page 199), if desired.

Calories	275	Calcium	261 mg
Calories from fat	23	Iron	1 mg
Total fat	3 g	Potassium	866 mg
Carbohydrates	72 g	Beta Carotene	1463 mcg
Protein	9 g	Magnesium	51 mg
Fiber	8 g	Folic Acid	36 mcg

Itsy Bitsy Cider

The sun's up and it's dried up all the rain—and it's time to indulge in this luscious blueberry and banana smoothie made with apple cider. But don't be a slave to the weatherman. Mix up a batch no matter what the forecast.

1 SERVING

½ cup apple cider

1 to 2 teaspoons honey (or to taste), optional

1 cup blueberries

½ cup diced banana

½ cup lowfat blueberry or nonfat vanilla frozen yogurt

Place all ingredients in a blender and mix by using the on/off pulse function until the ingredients are mostly blended. Continue mixing, gradually increasing the speed, until the mixture is smooth. Pour the smoothie into a glass and garnish with an Apple Chip (page 195), if desired.

Calories	291	Calcium	274 mg
Calories from fat	30	Iron	1 mg
Total fat	3 g	Potassium	592 mg
Carbohydrates	77 g	Beta Carotene	36 mcg
Protein	81 g	Magnesium	44 mg
Fiber	8 g	Folic Acid	28 mcg

Let There Be Lite

Hallelujah! This raspberry, peach, and banana smoothie is too divine for words. Enjoy this guilt-free indulgence whenever the temptation gets the best of you.

1 SERVING

½ cup unsweetened pineapple juice

1 to 2 teaspoons honey (or to taste), optional

½ cup diced peach

½ cup diced banana

½ cup raspberries

¼ cup lowfat raspberry or nonfat vanilla frozen yogurt

Place all ingredients in a blender and mix by using the on/off pulse function until the ingredients are mostly blended. Continue mixing, gradually increasing the speed, until the mixture is smooth. Pour the smoothie into a glass and garnish with a Pineapple Bow (page 207), if desired.

Calories	257	Calcium	120 mg
Calories from fat	14	Iron	1 mg
Total fat	2 g	Potassium	824 mg
Carbohydrates	61 g	Beta Carotene	289 mcg
Protein	5 g	Magnesium	62 mg
Fiber	8 g	Folic Acid	66 mcg

Meet the Pear-ents

You don't need anyone's permission to wed pears and bananas in a blissfully sweet smoothie. I promise, nothing could possibly go wrong when you introduce the folks to the wonders of this low-cal refreshment.

1 SERVING

½ cup pear nectar

1 to 2 teaspoons honey (or to taste), optional

⅛ teaspoon vanilla extract

1 cup diced pear

½ cup diced banana

¼ cup nonfat vanilla frozen yogurt

Place all ingredients in a blender and mix by using the on/off pulse function until the ingredients are mostly blended. Continue mixing, gradually increasing the speed, until the mixture is smooth. Pour the smoothie into a glass and garnish with Mint Leaves (page 205), if desired.

Calories	291	Calcium	113 mg
Calories from fat	10	Iron	1 mg
Total fat	1 g	Potassium	627 mg
Carbohydrates	72 g	Beta Carotene	57 mcg
Protein	4 g	Magnesium	43 mg
Fiber	7 g	Folic Acid	32 mcg

Melon of Troy

The taste that launched a thousand sips. There's no mythology to it, this cantaloupe, strawberry, and banana smoothie is a classic.

1 SERVING

½ cup peach nectar

1 to 2 teaspoons honey (or to taste), optional

½ cup diced cantaloupe

½ cup diced strawberries

½ cup diced banana

⅓ cup lowfat strawberry or nonfat vanilla frozen yogurt

Place all ingredients in a blender and mix by using the on/off pulse function until the ingredients are mostly blended. Continue mixing, gradually increasing the speed, until the mixture is smooth. Pour the smoothie into a glass and garnish with Melon Balls on a Skewer (page 204), if desired.

Calories	254	Calcium	132 mg
Calories from fat	16	Iron	1 mg
Total fat	2 g	Potassium	845 mg
Carbohydrates	59 g	Beta Carotene	1702 mcg
Protein	5 g	Magnesium	53 mg
Fiber	5 g	Folic Acid	49 mcg

Mr. Nectarine Man

Put a charge in your day by serving this nectarine smoothie in the jingle jangle of the morning. For an added taste sensation, spoon some of it over your favorite lowfat waffle.

1 SERVING

½ cup peach nectar

1 to 2 teaspoons honey (or to taste), optional

1 cup diced nectarine

½ cup diced banana

⅓ cup lowfat peach or nonfat vanilla frozen yogurt

Place all ingredients in a blender and mix by using the on/off pulse function until the ingredients are mostly blended. Continue mixing, gradually increasing the speed, until the mixture is smooth. Pour the smoothie into a glass and garnish the rim with a Lime Wheel (page 203), if desired.

Calories	272	Calcium	120 mg
Calories from fat	17	Iron	1 mg
Total fat	2 g	Potassium	770 mg
Carbohydrates	63 g	Beta Carotene	699 mcg
Protein	5 g	Magnesium	48 mg
Fiber	5 g	Folic Acid	27 mcg

Nect to Nothing

This nectarine smoothie is so light you'll never notice a difference when you step on the scale. Splurge on this sensational fruity concoction any time hunger strikes.

1 SERVING

½ cup apricot nectar

1 to 2 teaspoons honey (or to taste), optional

1 cup diced nectarine

½ cup diced banana

¼ cup lowfat banana or nonfat vanilla frozen yogurt

Place all ingredients in a blender and mix by using the on/off pulse function until the ingredients are mostly blended. Continue mixing, gradually increasing the speed, until the mixture is smooth. Pour the smoothie into a glass and garnish with a Kumquat Lily (page 202), if desired.

Calories	258	Calcium	97 mg
Calories from fat	16	Iron	1 mg
Total fat	2 g	Potassium	831 mg
Carbohydrates	61 g	Beta Carotene	1530 mcg
Protein	5 g	Magnesium	46 mg
Fiber	5 g	Folic Acid	26 mcg

Nobel Peach Prize

This cool indulgence bursting with rich peach and banana flavors is dynamite! Spoon some of this award-winning smoothie over a bowl of lowfat granola and watch the flavors explode.

1 SERVING

½ cup apricot nectar

1 to 2 teaspoons honey (or to taste), optional

1 cup diced peach

½ cup diced banana

¼ cup lowfat peach or nonfat vanilla frozen yogurt

Place all ingredients in a blender and mix by using the on/off pulse function until the ingredients are mostly blended. Continue mixing, gradually increasing the speed, until the mixture is smooth. Pour the smoothie into a glass and garnish with a Banana Wafer (page 197), if desired.

Calories	263	Calcium	99 mg
Calories from fat	11	Iron	1 mg
Total fat	1 g	Potassium	873 mg
Carbohydrates	64 g	Beta Carotene	1475 mcg
Protein	5 g	Magnesium	47 mg
Fiber	6 g	Folic Acid	25 mcg

Peach Volleyball

Ace your diet by serving this double-quick smoothie made with peaches, banana, and kiwi. Because it's low in calories, it's the perfect setup to assist you in netting guilt-free flavor satisfaction.

1 SERVING

½ cup peach nectar

1 to 2 teaspoons honey (or to taste), optional

½ cup diced peach

½ cup diced kiwi

½ cup diced banana

¼ cup lowfat strawberry or nonfat vanilla frozen yogurt

Place all ingredients in a blender and mix by using the on/off pulse function until the ingredients are mostly blended. Continue mixing, gradually increasing the speed, until the mixture is smooth. Pour the smoothie into a glass and garnish the rim with a Strawberry Fan (page 211), if desired.

Calories	278	Calcium	115 mg
Calories from fat	14	Iron	1 mg
Total fat	2 g	Potassium	906 mg
Carbohydrates	67 g	Beta Carotene	514 mcg
Protein	5 g	Magnesium	67 mg
Fiber	7 g	Folic Acid	56 mcg

Peel of Fortune

Spin some pineapple, orange, banana, and yogurt together in the blender and you'll solve the puzzle of great flavors with few calories. Invite friends over for an evening of games and serve glassfuls of this winning treat with an assortment of lowfat cookies.

1 SERVING

½ cup white cranberry juice

1 to 2 teaspoons honey (or to taste), optional

½ cup diced orange

½ cup diced pineapple

½ cup diced banana

¼ cup vanilla nonfat yogurt

Place all ingredients in a blender and mix by using the on/off pulse function until the ingredients are mostly blended. Continue mixing, gradually increasing the speed, until the mixture is smooth. Pour the smoothie into a glass and garnish the rim with an Orange Wheel (page 203), if desired.

Calories	259	Calcium	155 mg
Calories from fat	8	Iron	1 mg
Total fat	1 g	Potassium	687 mg
Carbohydrates	62 g	Beta Carotene	80 mcg
Protein	5 g	Magnesium	52 mg
Fiber	5 g	Folic Acid	57 mcg

Rasp-ody in Blue

By George! This jazzy raspberry, blueberry, and banana smoothie is poised to become an undisputed American classic. Reward yourself with a glassful after a run on the treadmill.

1 SERVING

½ cup unsweetened guava juice

1 to 2 teaspoons honey (or to taste), optional

½ cup raspberries

½ cup blueberries

½ cup diced banana

⅓ cup lowfat raspberry or nonfat vanilla frozen yogurt

Place all ingredients in a blender and mix by using the on/off pulse function until the ingredients are mostly blended. Continue mixing, gradually increasing the speed, until the mixture is smooth. Pour the smoothie into a glass and garnish with Berries on a Skewer (page 199), if desired.

Calories	257	Calcium	150 mg
Calories from fat	19	Iron	1 mg
Total fat	2 g	Potassium	522 mg
Carbohydrates	60 g	Beta Carotene	60 mcg
Protein	5 g	Magnesium	43 mg
Fiber	9 g	Folic Acid	37 mcg

Star Lite, Star Bright

Have your wish for something amazingly low in calories but dazzling in taste come true tonight by sampling a glass of this stellar peach, banana, apricot, and yogurt smoothie.

1 SERVING

¼ cup white cranberry juice

¼ cup lowfat (2 percent) milk

1 to 2 teaspoons honey (or to taste), optional

½ cup diced peach

½ cup diced banana

½ cup diced apricots

½ cup lowfat blueberry or nonfat vanilla frozen yogurt

Place all ingredients in a blender and mix by using the on/off pulse function until the ingredients are mostly blended. Continue mixing, gradually increasing the speed, until the mixture is smooth. Pour the smoothie into a glass and garnish with Mint Leaves (page 205), if desired.

Calories	304	Calcium	241 mg
Calories from fat	30	Iron	1 mg
Total fat	3 g	Potassium	993 mg
Carbohydrates	64 g	Beta Carotene	1469 mcg
Protein	9 g	Magnesium	49 mg
Fiber	5 g	Folic Acid	33 mcg

Thin City

There is nothing sinful about indulging in this seductively delicious strawberry and banana smoothie. It's the perfect guilt-free elixir to cool you down after an hour of intense power walking.

1 SERVING

½ cup apricot nectar

1 to 2 teaspoons honey (or to taste), optional

¾ cup diced banana

½ cup diced strawberries

¼ cup lowfat strawberry or nonfat vanilla frozen yogurt

Place all ingredients in a blender and mix by using the on/off pulse function until the ingredients are mostly blended. Continue mixing, gradually increasing the speed, until the mixture is smooth. Pour the smoothie into a glass and garnish the rim with a Strawberry Fan (page 211), if desired.

Calories	251	Calcium	103 mg
Calories from fat	14	Iron	1 mg
Total fat	2 g	Potassium	813 mg
Carbohydrates	59 g	Beta Carotene	1054 mcg
Protein	4 g	Magnesium	54 mg
Fiber	5 g	Folic Acid	41 mcg

Waist Not, Apricot

Enjoy this slimming apricot smoothie that's easy on your belt size and makes a simply delicious and healthful afternoon snack.

1 SERVING

½ cup unsweetened pineapple juice

1 to 2 teaspoons honey (or to taste), optional

1 cup diced apricots

½ cup diced banana

¼ cup lowfat banana or nonfat vanilla frozen yogurt

Place all ingredients in a blender and mix by using the on/off pulse function until the ingredients are mostly blended. Continue mixing, gradually increasing the speed, until the mixture is smooth. Pour the smoothie into a glass and garnish the rim with a Pineapple Spear (page 208), if desired.

Calories	264	Calcium	124 mg
Calories from fat	15	Iron	1 mg
Total fat	2 g	Potassium	1022 mg
Carbohydrates	61 g	Beta Carotene	2453 mcg
Protein	6 g	Magnesium	58 mg
Fiber	6 g	Folic Acid	62 mcg

What a Waist

Incorporate this low-cal blueberry, mango, and banana smoothie in your diet and watch your friends' amazement over your new slim shape. Share your secret with them after a brisk walk.

1 SERVING

½ cup unsweetened peach juice

1 to 2 teaspoons honey (or to taste), optional

½ cup blueberries

½ cup diced mango

½ cup diced banana

¼ cup nonfat vanilla frozen yogurt

Place all ingredients in a blender and mix by using the on/off pulse function until the ingredients are mostly blended. Continue mixing, gradually increasing the speed, until the mixture is smooth. Pour the smoothie into a glass and garnish with a Kumquat Lily (page 202), if desired.

Calories	260	Calcium	116 mg
Calories from fat	10	Iron	1 mg
Total fat	1 g	Potassium	532 mg
Carbohydrates	65 g	Beta Carotene	1962 mcg
Protein	4 g	Magnesium	37 mg
Fiber	6 g	Folic Acid	31 mcg

Yabba Dabba Blue

It's true! Archeological evidence has proven that Stone Age people enjoyed a cold smoothie after a hard day of hunting and gathering. Try this flavorful blueberry concoction and it will become a favorite in your cave.

1 SERVING

½ cup peach nectar

1 to 2 teaspoons honey (or to taste), optional

1 cup blueberries

½ cup diced banana

¼ cup lowfat blueberry yogurt

Place all ingredients in a blender and mix by using the on/off pulse function until the ingredients are mostly blended. Continue mixing, gradually increasing the speed, until the mixture is smooth. Pour the smoothie into a glass and garnish with Berries on a Skewer (page 199), if desired.

Calories	254	Calcium	126 mg
Calories from fat	18	Iron	1 mg
Total fat	2 g	Potassium	454 mg
Carbohydrates	63 g	Beta Carotene	193 mcg
Protein	4 g	Magnesium	27 mg
Fiber	9 g	Folic Acid	16 mcg

CHAPTER **6**

Fortified Smoothies

Smoothies have quickly become the "in" drink for people of all ages. These easy-to-prepare delights are especially appealing if you're counting calories or attempting to reduce the fat in your diet. Of course, it's easy to fall into the trap of eliminating too many healthful foods from your menu in the name of cutting back on calories and fat. Nearly all health experts agree that when trying to lose weight, it's important to eat a balanced diet of grains, fruits, and vegetables, and to include smaller servings of whole dairy products and meats. A well-conceived smoothie can be your ticket to reaching this goal and fulfilling the American Cancer Institute's recommendation to include at least two to three servings of fruit in your daily diet. What's more, these delicious taste sensations also can be an important source of protein and calcium when lowfat dairy products are added. As healthful as smoothies can be, they usually aren't considered a meal replacement, enjoyed instead as a nutritious low-cal snack or a supplement to a meal. However, on those occasions when you would like to transform a smoothie into an instant meal, there are a number of breakfast powders, protein supplements, nutritional boosters, herbs, and extracts that can be added to achieve this goal. (For a rundown of several health-promoting boosters that you can add to smoothies to provide benefits such as enhanced energy, improved memory, and relief from stress, see chapter 1.)

Another way to transform a smoothie into a still-healthier snack or meal is to prepare it with one or more soybean products, such as soy milk, tofu, or soy yogurt. These soy foods are not only good for you, but they also add unique and appealing flavors to a smoothie.

In this chapter, you will be delighted to find more than 40 recipes designed for the most health-conscious smoothie lovers among us. Two of my favorites are the flavorful wheat bran refresher Kukla, Bran, and Ollie (page 148) and the soy protein–enhanced Just You Whey, 'Enry 'Iggins (page 178). No matter which recipes become your favorites, you'll find that these fruity blends are a dieter's dream come true—rich in taste, nutritionally satisfying, and low enough in calories so you can indulge in them any time of the day. So come aboard and begin to experience the satisfaction of knowing that with every sip, you're doing something good for yourself.

SUPER LOW-CAL SMOOTHIES

These nutritious treats in a glass have 250 or fewer calories.

Shopping List

Fruit
Apricots
Bananas
Blackberries
Blueberries
Cantaloupe
Cherries
Mangoes

Oranges
Papayas
Peaches
Pineapple
Raspberries
Strawberries

Juice and Nectar
Orange juice
Peach nectar
Pear nectar
Unsweetened apple
    juice
Unsweetened guava
    juice

Unsweetened mango
    juice
Unsweetened peach
    juice
Unsweetened pine-
    apple juice
White cranberry juice

Miscellaneous
Bee pollen
Blueberry soy yogurt
Echinacea extract
    (optional)
Flaxseed oil
Ginkgo biloba extract
Ginseng extract
Honey (optional)

Nonfat blueberry
    yogurt
Nonfat milk
Nonfat nondairy
    vanilla soy beverage
    (or soy milk)
Raspberry sorbet
Raspberry soy yogurt

Soft silken-style tofu
Strawberry sorbet
Strawberry soy yogurt
Vanilla-flavored whey
    protein powder

Vitamin C powder
Wheat bran
Wheat germ

Ain't She Wheat

I ask you very confidentially, is this orange, pine-apple, and banana smoothie enhanced with wheat germ close to perfection? Serve this sweet tempta-tion as the centerpiece of a healthy breakfast.

1 SERVING

¼ cup nonfat nondairy vanilla soy beverage
   (or soy milk)

¼ cup orange juice

1 to 2 teaspoons honey (or to taste), optional

½ cup diced orange

½ cup diced pineapple

½ cup diced banana

2 tablespoons wheat germ

Place all ingredients in a blender and mix by using the on/off pulse function until the ingredients are mostly blended. Continue mixing, gradually increasing the speed, until the mixture is smooth. Pour the smoothie into a glass and garnish the rim with a Pineapple Bow (page 207), if desired.

Calories	238	Calcium	166 mg
Calories from fat	11	Iron	2 mg
Total fat	1 g	Potassium	760 mg
Carbohydrates	56 g	Beta Carotene	103 mcg
Protein	6 g	Magnesium	48 mg
Fiber	7 g	Folic Acid	69 mcg

Bananaconda

If you thought it was possible to squeeze a few more calories out of your diet, just slither over to the blender and try a glass of this low-cal banana, pineapple, and soy delight.

1 SERVING

¼ cup nonfat nondairy vanilla soy beverage (or soy milk)

¼ cup unsweetened pineapple juice

1 to 2 teaspoons honey (or to taste), optional

½ cup diced banana

¾ cup diced pineapple

⅓ cup soft silken-style tofu

Place all ingredients in a blender and mix by using the on/off pulse function until the ingredients are mostly blended. Continue mixing, gradually increasing the speed, until the mixture is smooth. Pour the smoothie into a glass and garnish the rim with a Pineapple Slice (page 208), if desired.

Calories	220	Calcium	149 mg
Calories from fat	27	Iron	2 mg
Total fat	3 g	Potassium	653 mg
Carbohydrates	52 g	Beta Carotene	51 mcg
Protein	7 g	Magnesium	68 mg
Fiber	5 g	Folic Acid	41 mcg

Bran Appétit!

Bonjour! You'll never rue the day you discovered how to start the morning with a generous helping of this bran-fortified papaya and banana smoothie. It's a smoothie work of art—Louvre gotta try it!

1 SERVING

¼ cup nonfat nondairy vanilla soy beverage (or soy milk)

¼ cup unsweetened mango juice

1 to 2 teaspoons honey (or to taste), optional

1 cup diced papaya

½ cup diced banana

¼ cup soft silken-style tofu

1 tablespoon wheat bran

Place all ingredients in a blender and mix by using the on/off pulse function until the ingredients are mostly blended. Continue mixing, gradually increasing the speed, until the mixture is smooth. Pour the smoothie into a glass and garnish with a Banana Wafer (page 197), if desired.

Calories	220	Calcium	183 mg
Calories from fat	20	Iron	2 mg
Total fat	2 g	Potassium	807 mg
Carbohydrates	48 g	Beta Carotene	106 mcg
Protein	54 g	Magnesium	74 mg
Fiber	6 g	Folic Acid	70 mcg

Fitness Protection Program

With all the pounds you'll shed after incorporating this ultra-low-cal soy and fruit pleaser in your diet, you may feel like you have an entirely new identity. Don't keep all this good news to yourself; feel free to testify to anyone about your FBI (Fabulous Beverage Innovation) connections.

1 SERVING

¼ cup nonfat nondairy vanilla soy beverage (or soy milk)

¼ cup unsweetened guava juice

1 to 2 teaspoons honey (or to taste), optional

½ cup diced orange

½ cup diced strawberries

½ cup diced banana

¼ cup strawberry soy yogurt

(continues)

Place all ingredients in a blender and mix by using the on/off pulse function until the ingredients are mostly blended. Continue mixing, gradually increasing the speed, until the mixture is smooth. Pour the smoothie into a glass and garnish the rim with a Strawberry Fan (page 211), if desired.

Calories	245	Calcium	323 mg
Calories from fat	13	Iron	1 mg
Total fat	1 g	Potassium	591 mg
Carbohydrates	57 g	Beta Carotene	83 mcg
Protein	5 g	Magnesium	38 mg
Fiber	6 g	Folic Acid	55 mcg

Flax-adaisical

Take your time savoring and enjoying this delicious flax-enriched combination of four fruit flavors. Enjoy it while winding down after a brisk walk.

1 SERVING

¼ cup nonfat nondairy vanilla soy beverage (or soy milk)

¼ cup white cranberry juice

1 to 2 teaspoons honey (or to taste), optional

½ cup diced strawberries

½ cup diced cherries

½ cup diced banana

2 tablespoons strawberry sorbet

1 tablespoon flaxseed oil (or according to specific-brand label recommendations)

Place all ingredients in a blender and mix by using the on/off pulse function until the ingredients are mostly blended. Continue mixing, gradually increasing the speed, until the mixture is smooth. Pour the smoothie into a glass and garnish the rim with a Strawberry Fan (page 211), if desired.

Calories	231	Calcium	126 mg
Calories from fat	12	Iron	1 mg
Total fat	1 g	Potassium	591 mg
Carbohydrates	55 g	Beta Carotene	132 mcg
Protein	4 g	Magnesium	37 mg
Fiber	6 g	Folic Acid	31 mcg

Flax Fifth Avenue

You can afford to indulge in this upscale pineapple, banana, apricot, and flax smoothie because it's low in calories, yet rich in taste and satisfaction. It's the perfect way to get ready for that weekend trip to the mall—and enjoy every drop until you shop.

1 SERVING

½ cup unsweetened pineapple juice

1 to 2 teaspoons honey (or to taste), optional

½ cup diced pineapple

½ cup diced banana

½ cup diced apricots

1 tablespoon flaxseed oil (or according to specific-brand label recommendations)

1 tablespoon bee pollen (or according to specific-brand label recommendations), optional

Ginseng extract (according to specific-brand label recommendations), optional

Ginkgo biloba extract (according to specific-brand label recommendations), optional

Place all ingredients in a blender and mix by using the on/off pulse function until the ingredients are mostly blended. Continue mixing, gradually increasing the speed, until the mixture is smooth. Pour the smoothie into a glass and garnish with a Kumquat Lily (page 202), if desired.

Calories	214	Calcium	42 mg
Calories from fat	10	Iron	1 mg
Total fat	1 g	Potassium	781 mg
Carbohydrates	53 g	Beta Carotene	1255 mcg
Protein	3 g	Magnesium	55 mg
Fiber	5 g	Folic Acid	59 mcg

From C to Shining C

If you feel like you're coming down with a cold, this majestic purple-colored blackberry, orange, and banana smoothie, enriched with vitamin C, will have you feeling better in no time.

1 SERVING

½ cup white cranberry juice

1 to 2 teaspoons honey (or to taste), optional

½ cup blackberries

½ cup diced orange

½ cup diced banana

¼ cup nonfat blueberry yogurt

1 tablespoon vitamin C powder (or according to specific-brand label recommendations)

Echinacea extract (according to specific-brand label recommendations), optional

Place all ingredients in a blender and mix by using the on/off pulse function until the ingredients are mostly blended. Continue mixing, gradually increasing the speed, until the mixture is smooth. Pour the smoothie into a glass and garnish the rim with an Orange Wheel (page 203), if desired.

Calories	233	Calcium	151 mg
Calories from fat	7	Iron	1 mg
Total fat	1 g	Potassium	691 mg
Carbohydrates	56 g	Beta Carotene	106 mcg
Protein	4 g	Magnesium	45 mg
Fiber	8 g	Folic Acid	66 mcg

How Wheat It Is

Start the morning with a glassful of this low calorie, fiber-rich combination of blueberries, pineapple, banana, soy, and wheat germ—and away you'll go.

1 SERVING

¼ cup nonfat nondairy vanilla soy beverage (or soy milk)

¼ cup orange juice

1 to 2 teaspoons honey (or to taste), optional

½ cup blueberries

½ cup diced pineapple

½ cup diced banana

1 to 2 tablespoons wheat germ

1 tablespoon flaxseed oil (or according to specific-brand label recommendations)

Place all ingredients in a blender and mix by using the on/off pulse function until the ingredients are mostly blended. Continue mixing, gradually increasing the speed, until the mixture is smooth. Pour the smoothie into a glass and garnish the rim with an Orange, Lemon, and Cherry Combo (page 206), if desired.

Calories	209	Calcium	143 mg
Calories from fat	13	Iron	2 mg
Total fat	1 g	Potassium	555 mg
Carbohydrates	51 g	Beta Carotene	68 mcg
Protein	5 g	Magnesium	39 mg
Fiber	7 g	Folic Acid	41 mcg

Jump for Soy

It will be hard to hide your excitement after sampling this strawberry, peach, and soy smoothie. What a delicious way to get a healthy dose of soy and fiber.

1 SERVING

¼ cup nonfat nondairy vanilla soy beverage (or soy milk)

¼ cup unsweetened peach juice

1 to 2 teaspoons honey (or to taste), optional

1 cup diced strawberries

½ cup diced peach

¼ cup strawberry soy yogurt

Place all ingredients in a blender and mix by using the on/off pulse function until the ingredients are mostly blended. Continue mixing, gradually increasing the speed, until the mixture is smooth. Pour the smoothie into a glass and garnish the rim with a Strawberry Fan (page 211), if desired.

Calories	193	Calcium	292 mg
Calories from fat	12	Iron	1 mg
Total fat	1 g	Potassium	425 mg
Carbohydrates	43 g	Beta Carotene	250 mcg
Protein	4 g	Magnesium	21 mg
Fiber	6 g	Folic Acid	30 mcg

Just the Flax, Ma'am

Serve this flax-enriched pleaser to your health-conscious friends on Friday—or any other day of the week—and you'll live up to your reputation as a good Joe (or Jane).

1 SERVING

½ cup unsweetened peach juice

1 to 2 teaspoons honey (or to taste), optional

½ cup diced peach

½ cup diced cantaloupe

½ cup diced banana

¼ cup soft silken-style tofu

1 tablespoon flaxseed oil (or according to specific-brand label recommendations)

Place all ingredients in a blender and mix by using the on/off pulse function until the ingredients are mostly blended. Continue mixing, gradually increasing the speed, until the mixture is smooth. Pour the smoothie into a glass and garnish the rim with a Star Fruit Slice (page 210), if desired.

Calories	224	Calcium	35 mg
Calories from fat	20	Iron	1 mg
Total fat	2 g	Potassium	808 mg
Carbohydrates	50 g	Beta Carotene	1759 mcg
Protein	5 g	Magnesium	53 mg
Fiber	4 g	Folic Acid	30 mcg

Kukla, Bran, and Ollie

If your diet has you "dragon," try a glass of this classic fiber-enriched raspberry, cantaloupe, and banana smoothie for an energy boost. Spoon a dollop on your cereal or have it as a midday snack. It's the perfect helping hand.

1 SERVING

½ cup orange juice

2 tablespoons nonfat nondairy vanilla soy beverage (or soy milk)

1 to 2 teaspoons honey (or to taste), optional

½ cup raspberries

½ cup diced cantaloupe

½ cup diced banana

1 tablespoon wheat bran

1 tablespoon wheat germ

Place all ingredients in a blender and mix by using the on/off pulse function until the ingredients are mostly blended. Continue mixing, gradually increasing the speed, until the mixture is smooth. Pour the smoothie into a glass and garnish with Melon Balls on a Skewer (page 204), if desired.

Calories	220	Calcium	100 mg
Calories from fat	13	Iron	2 mg
Total fat	1 g	Potassium	967 mg
Carbohydrates	53 g	Beta Carotene	1604 mcg
Protein	5 g	Magnesium	77 mg
Fiber	9 g	Folic Acid	84 mcg

Lean Dancing

Take a "Little Stroll" over to your blender and whip up this strawberry and banana smoothie. One taste and you'll want to "Twist and Stomp" all night.

1 SERVING

½ cup orange juice

1 to 2 teaspoons honey (or to taste), optional

1 cup diced strawberries

½ cup diced banana

1 tablespoon wheat bran

1 tablespoon wheat germ

Place all ingredients in a blender and mix by using the on/off pulse function until the ingredients are mostly blended. Continue mixing, gradually increasing the speed, until the mixture is smooth. Pour the smoothie into a glass and garnish with a Banana Wafer (page 197), if desired.

Calories	195	Calcium	49 mg
Calories from fat	13	Iron	2 mg
Total fat	1 g	Potassium	882 mg
Carbohydrates	47 g	Beta Carotene	107 mcg
Protein	4 g	Magnesium	73 mg
Fiber	8 g	Folic Acid	82 mcg

Let It Bee

Whether you find yourself in happy moments or times of trouble, try indulging in this pollen-enhanced raspberry and banana smoothie, and there will "bee" an answer.

1 SERVING

¼ cup nonfat or lowfat milk

¼ cup unsweetened apple juice

1 to 2 teaspoons honey (or to taste), optional

1 cup raspberries

½ cup diced banana

¼ cup raspberry sorbet

1 tablespoon bee pollen (or according to specific-brand label recommendations)

Place all ingredients in a blender and mix by using the on/off pulse function until the ingredients are mostly blended. Continue mixing, gradually increasing the speed, until the mixture is smooth. Pour the smoothie into a glass and garnish with an Apple Chip (page 195), if desired.

Calories	241	Calcium	103 mg
Calories from fat	10	Iron	1 mg
Total fat	1 g	Potassium	686 mg
Carbohydrates	57 g	Beta Carotene	84 mcg
Protein	4 g	Magnesium	46 mg
Fiber	11 g	Folic Acid	46 mcg

Michael Flax-son

If you're looking for a smoothie that's a real "Thriller," then "Beat It" to the blender and whip up this fabulous concoction made with blueberries, banana, pineapple, flaxseed oil, and wheat germ.

1 SERVING

¼ cup nonfat nondairy vanilla soy beverage (or soy milk)

¼ cup orange juice

1 to 2 teaspoons honey (or to taste), optional

½ cup blueberries

½ cup diced pineapple

½ cup diced banana

1 tablespoon flaxseed oil (or according to specific-brand label recommendations)

1 to 2 tablespoons wheat germ

Place all ingredients in a blender and mix by using the on/off pulse function until the ingredients are mostly blended. Continue mixing, gradually increasing the speed, until the mixture is smooth. Pour the smoothie into a glass and garnish the rim with a Pineapple Bow (page 207), if desired.

Calories	209	Calcium	143 mg
Calories from fat	13	Iron	2 mg
Total fat	1 g	Potassium	555 mg
Carbohydrates	51 g	Beta Carotene	68 mcg
Protein	5 g	Magnesium	39 mg
Fiber	7 g	Folic Acid	41 mcg

Papaya New Skinny

Tired of those ordinary Polynesian smoothies? Margaret says try this exotic papaya creation and see if you don't notice your taste "growing up in new skinny."

1 SERVING

¼ cup nonfat nondairy vanilla soy beverage (or soy milk)

¼ cup unsweetened guava juice

1 to 2 teaspoons honey (or to taste), optional

1 cup diced pineapple

½ cup diced papaya

⅓ cup soft silken-style tofu

Place all ingredients in a blender and mix by using the on/off pulse function until the ingredients are mostly blended. Continue mixing, gradually increasing the speed, until the mixture is smooth. Pour the smoothie into a glass and garnish the rim with an Orange, Lemon, and Cherry Combo (page 206), if desired.

Calories	202	Calcium	156 mg
Calories from fat	25	Iron	2 mg
Total fat	3 g	Potassium	496 mg
Carbohydrates	41 g	Beta Carotene	53 mcg
Protein	6 g	Magnesium	51 mg
Fiber	3 g	Folic Acid	44 mcg

Ray-Bran

Shades of blueberries and cherries! You'll look so cool downing a glass of this fashionable bran-fortified smoothie. Enjoy this healthy taste treat after a brisk walk in the morning.

1 SERVING

¼ cup nonfat nondairy vanilla soy beverage (or soy milk)

¼ cup pear nectar

1 to 2 teaspoons honey (or to taste), optional

½ cup blueberries

¼ cup diced cherries

½ cup diced banana

¼ cup raspberry soy yogurt

1 tablespoon wheat bran

Place all ingredients in a blender and mix by using the on/off pulse function until the ingredients are mostly blended. Continue mixing, gradually increasing the speed, until the mixture is smooth. Pour the smoothie into a glass and garnish with a Pineapple Bow (page 207), if desired.

Calories	250	Calcium	302 mg
Calories from fat	18	Iron	2 mg
Total fat	2 g	Potassium	434 mg
Carbohydrates	60 g	Beta Carotene	98 mcg
Protein	5 g	Magnesium	50 mg
Fiber	8 g	Folic Acid	19 mcg

Rind over Matter

If you're craving something sweet right now, take control of your diet by willing a glassful of this low-calorie orange, strawberry, and banana smoothie to appear. Its rich flavor and smooth texture spell instant satisfaction.

1 SERVING

½ cup orange juice

1 to 2 teaspoons honey (or to taste), optional

½ cup diced orange

½ cup diced strawberries

½ cup diced banana

¼ cup strawberry soy yogurt

Place all ingredients in a blender and mix by using the on/off pulse function until the ingredients are mostly blended. Continue mixing, gradually increasing the speed, until the mixture is smooth. Pour the smoothie into a glass and garnish with a Kumquat Lily (page 202), if desired.

Calories	243	Calcium	231 mg
Calories from fat	15	Iron	1 mg
Total fat	2 g	Potassium	834 mg
Carbohydrates	57 g	Beta Carotene	130 mcg
Protein	4 g	Magnesium	52 mg
Fiber	6 g	Folic Acid	92 mcg

Rip Van Ginkgo

Whether your search for the ideal healthy smoothie has been going on for forty minutes or forty years, wake up to the flavor of this peach, banana, and apricot smoothie fortified with lots of boosters. It's the perfect eye-opener first thing in the morning.

1 SERVING

½ cup peach nectar

1 to 2 teaspoons honey (or to taste), optional

½ cup diced peach

½ cup diced banana

½ cup diced apricots

Ginkgo biloba extract (according to specific-brand label recommendations)

Ginseng extract (according to specific-brand label recommendations)

1 tablespoon flaxseed oil (or according to specific-brand label recommendations)

1 to 2 tablespoons wheat germ

Place all ingredients in a blender and mix by using the on/off pulse function until the ingredients are mostly blended. Continue mixing, gradually increasing the speed, until the mixture is smooth. Pour the smoothie into a glass and garnish with Mint Leaves (page 205), if desired.

Calories	227	Calcium	32 mg
Calories from fat	8	Iron	2 mg
Total fat	1 g	Potassium	785 mg
Carbohydrates	56 g	Beta Carotene	1625 mcg
Protein	4 g	Magnesium	39 mg
Fiber	7 g	Folic Acid	25 mcg

Soy-onara

Bring a pitcher of this richly flavored, soy-enhanced smoothie to work and have a Nippon your break. Once you become oriented to this wonderful healthful snack, it's goodbye to the fat and sugar-laden variety.

1 SERVING

¼ cup nonfat nondairy vanilla soy beverage (or soy milk)

¼ cup unsweetened mango juice

1 to 2 teaspoons honey (or to taste), optional

½ cup blueberries

½ cup diced apricots

¼ cup diced banana

¼ cup blueberry soy yogurt

Place all ingredients in a blender and mix by using the on/off pulse function until the ingredients are mostly blended. Continue mixing, gradually increasing the speed, until the mixture is smooth. Pour the smoothie into a glass and garnish with Berries on a Skewer (page 199), if desired.

Calories	213	Calcium	325 mg
Calories from fat	15	Iron	1 mg
Total fat	2 g	Potassium	383 mg
Carbohydrates	49 g	Beta Carotene	1225 mcg
Protein	52 g	Magnesium	17 mg
Fiber	7 g	Folic Acid	14 mcg

Soy Crazy

You'll giggle over the sensational, flirty taste of this strawberry, banana, and soy smoothie. Invite someone special over to share this heartthrob in a glass, and marvel over its romantic blush color.

1 SERVING

¼ cup nonfat nondairy vanilla soy beverage (or soy milk)

¼ cup peach nectar

1 to 2 teaspoons honey (or to taste), optional

1 cup diced strawberries

½ cup diced banana

⅓ cup soft silken-style tofu

Place all ingredients in a blender and mix by using the on/off pulse function until the ingredients are mostly blended. Continue mixing, gradually increasing the speed, until the mixture is smooth. Pour the smoothie into a glass and garnish the rim with a Strawberry Fan (page 211), if desired.

Calories	217	Calcium	152 mg
Calories from fat	27	Iron	2 mg
Total fat	3 g	Potassium	715 mg
Carbohydrates	45 g	Beta Carotene	139 mcg
Protein	7 g	Magnesium	61 mg
Fiber	6 g	Folic Acid	42 mcg

The Whey You Look Tonight

You won't ever want to change the ingredients in this whey-fortified cherry and banana smoothie because it's perfect just the way it is. Enjoy this low-calorie taste sensation with a special someone who shares your love of looking and feeling great.

1 SERVING

½ cup unsweetened guava juice

1 to 2 teaspoons honey (or to taste), optional

¾ cup diced cherries

⅓ cup diced banana

1 tablespoon vanilla-flavored whey protein powder

Place all ingredients in a blender and mix by using the on/off pulse function until the ingredients are mostly blended. Continue mixing, gradually increasing the speed, until the mixture is smooth. Pour the smoothie into a glass and garnish the rim with an Orange, Lemon, and Cherry Combo (page 206), if desired.

Calories	220	Calcium	148 mg
Calories from fat	11	Iron	3 mg
Total fat	2 g	Potassium	268 mg
Carbohydrates	33 g	Beta Carotene	126 mcg
Protein	13 g	Magnesium	56 mg
Fiber	4 g	Folic Acid	49 mcg

Wheat Sixteen

Try this nutritiously satisfying smoothie and see if the amazing energy boost from its wheat germ and wheat bran doesn't result in at least "sixteen can-do's."

1 SERVING

¼ cup nonfat nondairy vanilla soy beverage (or soy milk)

¼ cup orange juice

1 to 2 teaspoons honey (or to taste), optional

½ cup diced apricots

½ cup diced mango

½ cup diced pineapple

1 tablespoon wheat bran

1 tablespoon wheat germ

Place all ingredients in a blender and mix by using the on/off pulse function until the ingredients are mostly blended. Continue mixing, gradually increasing the speed, until the mixture is smooth. Pour the smoothie into a glass and garnish the rim with an Orange Wheel (page 203), if desired.

Calories	209	Calcium	141 mg
Calories from fat	12	Iron	2 mg
Total fat	1 g	Potassium	659 mg
Carbohydrates	50 g	Beta Carotene	3164 mcg
Protein	5 g	Magnesium	53 mg
Fiber	7 g	Folic Acid	49 mcg

LOW-CAL SMOOTHIES

These delightful smoothies have 350 or fewer calories.

Shopping List

Fruit

Apricots
Bananas
Blackberries
Blueberries
Cantaloupe
Cherries
Kiwifruit
Mangos

Nectarines
Oranges
Peaches
Pears
Pineapple
Raspberries
Strawberries

Juice and nectar

Apricot nectar
Mango nectar
Orange juice
Peach nectar
Pear nectar
Unsweetened apple
  juice

Unsweetened mango
  juice
Unsweetened peach
  juice
White cranberry juice

Miscellaneous

Apricot-mango soy
  yogurt
Bee pollen
Blueberry soy yogurt
Cherry soy yogurt
Chocolate Soy Dream
  nondairy frozen
  dessert

Chocolate soy milk
Flaxseed oil
French vanilla Soy
  Dream nondairy
  frozen dessert
Gingko biloba extract
Ginseng extract
Honey (optional)

Nonfat nondairy vanilla soy beverage (or soy milk)

Peach soy yogurt

Raspberry soy yogurt

Soft silken-style tofu

Strawberry soy yogurt

Vanilla silk soy milk

Vanilla-flavored whey protein powder

Wheat bran

Wheat germ

As the Whirl Turns

There's nothing scandalous about indulging in this pineapple, orange, and banana smoothie. It is deceptively low in calories, seductively rich in flavor, and fortified with boosters. After one taste, you are destined to fall hopelessly in love with it.

1 SERVING

¼ cup nonfat nondairy vanilla soy beverage (or soy milk)

¼ cup orange juice

1 to 2 teaspoons honey (or to taste), optional

½ cup diced pineapple

½ cup diced orange

½ cup diced banana

⅓ cup soft silken-style tofu

1 to 2 tablespoons wheat germ

1 tablespoon flaxseed oil (or according to specific-brand label recommendations)

Gingko biloba extract (according to specific-brand label recommendations)

Ginseng extract (according to specific-brand label recommendations)

Place all ingredients in a blender and mix by using the on/off pulse function until the ingredients are mostly blended. Continue mixing, gradually increasing the speed, until the mixture is smooth. Pour the smoothie into a glass and garnish the rim with an Orange Wheel (page 203), if desired.

Calories	263	Calcium	183 mg
Calories from fat	28	Iron	2 mg
Total fat	3 g	Potassium	854 mg
Carbohydrates	55 g	Beta Carotene	103 mcg
Protein	8 g	Magnesium	70 mg
Fiber	6 g	Folic Acid	69 mcg

Back Street Soys

"It's True!" You'll adore this soy-fortified peach and banana smoothie. If you're looking for a pre-exercise energizer, it's "The One" to have before heading out to the tennis courts.

1 SERVING

¼ cup nonfat nondairy vanilla soy beverage (or soy milk)

¼ cup peach nectar

1 to 2 teaspoons honey (or to taste), optional

1 cup diced peach

½ cup diced banana

⅓ cup French vanilla Soy Dream nondairy frozen dessert

Place all ingredients in a blender and mix by using the on/off pulse function until the ingredients are mostly blended. Continue mixing, gradually increasing the speed, until the mixture is smooth. Pour the smoothie into a glass and garnish with Mint Leaves (page 205), if desired.

Calories	326	Calcium	116 mg
Calories from fat	60	Iron	1 mg
Total fat	7 g	Potassium	662 mg
Carbohydrates	65 g	Beta Carotene	566 mcg
Protein	5 g	Magnesium	36 mg
Fiber	7 g	Folic Acid	20 mcg

Britney Pears

Serve this healthful soy-enriched pear smoothie and you'll be creating a deep cleavage between yourself and those other people who prefer high-calorie, fat-laden drinks.

1 SERVING

¼ cup nonfat nondairy vanilla soy beverage (or soy milk)

¼ cup pear nectar

1 to 2 teaspoons honey (or to taste), optional

1 cup diced pear

¼ cup diced banana

¼ cup French vanilla Soy Dream nondairy frozen dessert

1 tablespoon bee pollen (or according to specific-brand label recommendations), optional

1 tablespoon flaxseed oil (or according to specific-brand label recommendations), optional

1 tablespoon ginseng extract (or according to specific-brand label recommendations), optional

(continues)

Place all ingredients in a blender and mix by using the on/off pulse function until the ingredients are mostly blended. Continue mixing, gradually increasing the speed, until the mixture is smooth. Pour the smoothie into a glass and garnish with a Kumquat Lily (page 202), if desired.

Calories	289	Calcium	124 mg
Calories from fat	49	Iron	1 mg
Total fat	5 g	Potassium	368 mg
Carbohydrates	60 g	Beta Carotene	38 mcg
Protein	3 g	Magnesium	23 mg
Fiber	6 g	Folic Acid	19 mcg

Cirque du Soy-leil

O! This smoothie, featuring cherries, blackberries, and banana outperforms most other healthful blends with its daring addition of soy.

1 SERVING

¼ cup nonfat nondairy vanilla soy beverage (or soy milk)

¼ cup white cranberry juice

1 to 2 teaspoons honey (or to taste), *optional*

½ cup diced cherries

½ cup blackberries

½ cup diced banana

⅓ cup French vanilla Soy Dream nondairy frozen dessert

Place all ingredients in a blender and mix by using the on/off pulse function until the ingredients are mostly blended. Continue mixing, gradually increasing the speed, until the mixture is smooth. Pour the smoothie into a glass and garnish with a Pineapple Bow (page 207), if desired.

Calories	336	Calcium	138 mg
Calories from fat	67	Iron	1 mg
Total fat	7 g	Potassium	606 mg
Carbohydrates	66 g	Beta Carotene	155 mcg
Protein	5 g	Magnesium	44 mg
Fiber	8 g	Folic Acid	42 mcg

Eight Days a Wheat

With the energizing jolt you'll get from this pineapple, blackberry, and banana smoothie, boosted with wheat germ and wheat bran, you'll feel Fab Five times more often than you ever have before.

1 SERVING

¼ cup nonfat nondairy vanilla soy beverage (or soy milk)

¼ cup white cranberry juice

1 to 2 teaspoons honey (or to taste), optional

½ cup diced pineapple

½ cup blackberries

½ cup diced banana

2 tablespoons blueberry soy yogurt

1 tablespoon wheat bran

1 tablespoon wheat germ

Place all ingredients in a blender and mix by using the on/off pulse function until the ingredients are mostly blended. Continue mixing, gradually increasing the speed, until the mixture is smooth. Pour the smoothie into a glass and garnish with a Banana Wafer (page 197), if desired.

Calories	251	Calcium	226 mg
Calories from fat	15	Iron	2 mg
Total fat	2 g	Potassium	615 mg
Carbohydrates	59 g	Beta Carotene	80 mcg
Protein	5 g	Magnesium	69 mg
Fiber	9 g	Folic Acid	50 mcg

Ginkgo, Drinkin', and Nod

Invite two friends over to share this gingko-enriched pineapple, kiwi, and banana smoothie, and don't be surprised if the entire threesome nod their heads in agreement that it's an unforgettable taste sensation. Wooden shoe agree?

1 SERVING

½ cup pear nectar

1 to 2 teaspoons honey (or to taste), optional

½ cup diced pineapple

½ cup diced kiwi

½ cup diced banana

⅓ cup soft silken-style tofu

¼ cup apricot-mango soy yogurt

Ginkgo biloba extract (according to specific-brand label recommendations), optional

(continues)

Place all ingredients in a blender and mix by using the on/off pulse function until the ingredients are mostly blended. Continue mixing, gradually increasing the speed, until the mixture is smooth. Pour the smoothie into a glass and garnish the rim with a Pineapple Wedge (page 208), if desired.

Calories	331	Calcium	229 mg
Calories from fat	34	Iron	2 mg
Total fat	4 g	Potassium	830 mg
Carbohydrates	72 g	Beta Carotene	141 mcg
Protein	7 g	Magnesium	85 mg
Fiber	7 g	Folic Acid	58 mcg

Got Silk?

To avoid getting a soy mustache, be sure to drink this mango and banana smoothie with a straw. For an extra taste treat, spoon some of this silky delight over a bowl of lowfat granola.

1 SERVING

¼ cup vanilla Silk soy milk

¼ cup mango nectar

1 to 2 teaspoons honey (or to taste), optional

1 cup diced mango

½ cup diced banana

⅓ cup apricot-mango soy yogurt

Place all ingredients in a blender and mix by using the on/off pulse function until the ingredients are mostly blended. Continue mixing, gradually increasing the speed, until the mixture is smooth. Pour the smoothie into a glass and garnish with Mint Leaves (page 205), if desired.

Calories	309	Calcium	321 mg
Calories from fat	24	Iron	1 mg
Total fat	3 g	Potassium	660 mg
Carbohydrates	71 g	Beta Carotene	4325 mcg
Protein	5 g	Magnesium	39 mg
Fiber	6 g	Folic Acid	45 mcg

It's Soy Easy

You'll fall in love with this peach, pineapple, and banana smoothie enhanced with soy and flaxseed oil. Invite a Buddy over, and, for a special touch, pour frosty portions of this taste sensation into black-rimmed glasses.

1 SERVING

¼ cup nonfat nondairy vanilla soy beverage (or soy milk)

¼ cup apricot nectar

1 to 2 teaspoons honey (or to taste), optional

½ cup diced peach

½ cup diced pineapple

½ cup diced banana

¼ cup peach soy yogurt

1 tablespoon flaxseed oil (or according to specific-brand label recommendations), optional

Place all ingredients in a blender and mix by using the on/off pulse function until the ingredients are mostly blended. Continue mixing, gradually increasing the speed, until the mixture is smooth. Pour the smoothie into a glass and garnish the rim with an Orange, Lemon, and Cherry Combo (page 206), if desired.

Calories	263	Calcium	285 mg
Calories from fat	13	Iron	1 mg
Total fat	1 g	Potassium	629 mg
Carbohydrates	62 g	Beta Carotene	765 mcg
Protein	5 g	Magnesium	42 mg
Fiber	5 g	Folic Acid	26 mcg

Johnny Bee Goode

If you're looking for great-tasting, high-energy re-freshment, then try this Berry special blueberry, peach, and banana smoothie Chuck-full of bee pollen, ginkgo, and ginseng.

1 SERVING

¼ cup nonfat nondairy vanilla soy beverage (or soy milk)

¼ cup unsweetened peach juice

1 to 2 teaspoons honey (or to taste), optional

½ cup blueberries

½ cup diced peach

½ cup diced banana

⅓ cup strawberry soy yogurt

1 tablespoon bee pollen (or according to specific-brand label recommendations)

Gingko biloba extract (according to specific-brand label recommendations)

Ginseng extract (according to specific-brand label recommendations)

Place all ingredients in a blender and mix by using the on/off pulse function until the ingredients are mostly blended. Continue mixing, gradually increasing the speed, until the mixture is smooth. Pour the smoothie into a glass and garnish with Berries on a Skewer (page 199), if desired.

Calories	264	Calcium	350 mg
Calories from fat	16	Iron	1 mg
Total fat	2 g	Potassium	469 mg
Carbohydrates	62 g	Beta Carotene	262 mcg
Protein	5 g	Magnesium	28 mg
Fiber	7 g	Folic Acid	17 mcg

Just You Whey, 'Enry 'Iggins

If you've been known to Doolittle to stay on a diet, try this cherry and banana smoothie enhanced with whey, and see if you don't become one of the healthiest people On the Street Where You Live.

1 SERVING

¼ cup nonfat nondairy vanilla soy beverage (or soy milk)

¼ cup unsweetened apple juice

1 to 2 teaspoons honey (or to taste), optional

1 cup diced cherries

½ cup diced banana

2 tablespoons cherry soy yogurt

1 tablespoon vanilla-flavored whey protein powder

Place all ingredients in a blender and mix by using the on/off pulse function until the ingredients are mostly blended. Continue mixing, gradually increasing the speed, until the mixture is smooth. Pour the smoothie into a glass and garnish with an Apple Chip (page 195), if desired.

Calories	304	Calcium	332 mg
Calories from fat	19	Iron	4 mg
Total fat	2 g	Potassium	743 mg
Carbohydrates	59 g	Beta Carotene	204 mcg
Protein	17 g	Magnesium	87 mg
Fiber	6 g	Folic Acid	68 mcg

Little Soy Blue

Start the morning with a tumblerful of this energizing smoothie made with soy products accented with the flavors of blueberry and banana, and you'll never be caught sleeping on the job.

1 SERVING

¼ cup nonfat nondairy vanilla soy beverage
  (or soy milk)

¼ cup unsweetened apple juice

1 to 2 teaspoons honey (or to taste), optional

1 cup blueberries

½ cup diced banana

⅓ cup soft silken-style tofu

¼ cup blueberry soy yogurt

Place all ingredients in a blender and mix by using the on/off pulse function until the ingredients are mostly blended. Continue mixing, gradually increasing the speed, until the mixture is smooth. Pour the smoothie into a glass and garnish with a Kumquat Lily (page 202), if desired.

Calories	280	Calcium	339 mg
Calories from fat	37	Iron	2 mg
Total fat	4 g	Potassium	512 mg
Carbohydrates	59 g	Beta Carotene	36 mcg
Protein	8 g	Magnesium	45 mg
Fiber	9 g	Folic Acid	14 mcg

Mariah Cherry

Put some "Glitter" in your day by making sure you're "Never Too Far" from a blender, and you can easily whip up a batch of this sensational cherry, mango, and soy smoothie. Enjoy this highly energizing fruit and soy "Twister" whenever you have a craving for something delicious and satisfying.

1 SERVING

¼ cup nonfat nondairy vanilla soy beverage
   (or soy milk)

¼ cup mango nectar

1 to 2 teaspoons honey (or to taste), optional

1 cup diced mango

½ cup diced cherries

⅓ cup cherry soy yogurt

Place all ingredients in a blender and mix by using the on/off pulse function until the ingredients are mostly blended. Continue mixing, gradually increasing the speed, until the mixture is smooth. Pour the smoothie into a glass and garnish the rim with a Pineapple Spear (page 208), if desired.

Calories	294	Calcium	352 mg
Calories from fat	19	Iron	1 mg
Total fat	2 g	Potassium	460 mg
Carbohydrates	68 g	Beta Carotene	4373 mcg
Protein	5 g	Magnesium	25 mg
Fiber	6 g	Folic Acid	28 mcg

Milky Whey

You'll be impressed by the heavenly delicious taste of this soy milk, orange, banana, apricot, and whey smoothie. Start off your next **Star Trek** *party with a big bang by serving glassfuls of this wonderful refreshment. Your friends will agree it's out of this world.*

1 SERVING

¼ cup nonfat nondairy vanilla soy beverage (or soy milk)

¼ cup orange juice

1 to 2 teaspoons honey (or to taste), optional

½ cup diced orange

½ cup diced apricots

½ cup diced banana

1 tablespoon vanilla-flavored whey protein powder

1 tablespoon wheat bran

Place all ingredients in a blender and mix by using the on/off pulse function until the ingredients are mostly blended. Continue mixing, gradually increasing the speed, until the mixture is smooth. Pour the smoothie into a glass and garnish the rim with an Orange Wheel (page 203), if desired.

Calories	259	Calcium	279 mg
Calories from fat	9	Iron	4 mg
Total fat	1 g	Potassium	904 mg
Carbohydrates	51 g	Beta Carotene	1301 mcg
Protein	17 g	Magnesium	113 mg
Fiber	8 g	Folic Acid	117 mcg

Ode to Soy

You'd have to be hard of hearing not to appreciate the chorus of rave reviews after you serve this fruit and soy masterpiece to friends.

1 SERVING

½ cup nonfat nondairy vanilla soy beverage (or soy milk)

1 to 2 teaspoons honey (or to taste), optional

½ cup blueberries

½ cup blackberries

½ cup diced banana

⅓ cup soft silken-style tofu

3 tablespoons blueberry soy yogurt

Place all ingredients in a blender and mix by using the on/off pulse function until the ingredients are mostly blended. Continue mixing, gradually increasing the speed, until the mixture is smooth. Pour the smoothie into a glass and garnish with Berries on a Skewer (page 199), if desired.

Calories	273	Calcium	396 mg
Calories from fat	33	Iron	2 mg
Total fat	4 g	Potassium	584 mg
Carbohydrates	56 g	Beta Carotene	71 mcg
Protein	9 g	Magnesium	58 mg
Fiber	9 g	Folic Acid	39 mcg

Pour Little Rich Whirl

Shirley a smoothie that is made with soy, nectarine, orange, banana, ginseng, ginkgo, and flaxseed oil has to be good for you. Oh my goodness, you just have to give this classic smoothie a try.

1 SERVING

¼ cup nonfat nondairy vanilla soy beverage (or soy milk)

¼ cup pear nectar

1 to 2 teaspoons honey (or to taste), optional

½ cup diced nectarine

½ cup diced orange

½ cup diced banana

⅓ cup soft silken-style tofu

Ginseng extract (according to specific-brand label recommendations)

Ginkgo biloba extract (according to specific-brand label recommendations), optional

1 tablespoon flaxseed oil (or according to specific-brand label recommendations), optional

(continues)

Place all ingredients in a blender and mix by using the on/off pulse function until the ingredients are mostly blended. Continue mixing, gradually increasing the speed, until the mixture is smooth. Pour the smoothie into a glass and garnish the rim with an Orange, Lemon, and Cherry Combo (page 206), if desired.

Calories	252	Calcium	170 mg
Calories from fat	25	Iron	2 mg
Total fat	3 g	Potassium	755 mg
Carbohydrates	54 g	Beta Carotene	325 mcg
Protein	7 g	Magnesium	60 mg
Fiber	6 g	Folic Acid	45 mcg

Sip a Soy, Mate

It will be smooth sailing when you dive into this cantaloupe, banana, and soy smoothie. Discover its great flavors before heading out for a day on the water.

1 SERVING

¼ cup nonfat nondairy vanilla soy beverage (or soy milk)

¼ cup mango nectar

1 to 2 teaspoons honey (or to taste), optional

1 cup diced cantaloupe

½ cup diced banana

⅓ cup French vanilla Soy Dream nondairy frozen dessert

Place all ingredients in a blender and mix by using the on/off pulse function until the ingredients are mostly blended. Continue mixing, gradually increasing the speed, until the mixture is smooth. Pour the smoothie into a glass and garnish with Melon Balls on a Skewer (page 204), if desired.

Calories	310	Calcium	125 mg
Calories from fat	63	Iron	1 mg
Total fat	7 g	Potassium	819 mg
Carbohydrates	60 g	Beta Carotene	3469 mcg
Protein	5 g	Magnesium	41 mg
Fiber	5 g	Folic Acid	43 mcg

Soy in Love with Chocolate

Who says you can't have chocolate when you're on a diet? Not only is this chocolate smoothie sweet and delicious, it's made with wholesome soybean products, so it's good for you, too. Enjoy!

1 SERVING

½ cup chocolate soy milk

½ cup diced banana

½ cup chocolate Soy Dream nondairy frozen dessert

Place all ingredients in a blender and mix by using the on/off pulse function until the ingredients are mostly blended. Continue mixing, gradually increasing the speed, until the mixture is smooth. Pour the smoothie into a glass and garnish with a Banana Wafer (page 197), if desired.

To make a chocolate–peanut butter smoothie, follow the instructions for Soy in Love with Chocolate using the following ingredients: ½ cup chocolate soy milk, ½ cup diced banana, 1 tablespoon reduced-fat natural peanut butter, and ¼ cup chocolate Soy Dream nondairy frozen dessert.

Calories	254	Calcium	155 mg
Calories from fat	71	Iron	1 mg
Total fat	8 g	Potassium	472 mg
Carbohydrates	44 g	Beta Carotene	36 mcg
Protein	4 g	Magnesium	22 mg
Fiber	3 g	Folic Acid	26 mcg

Soy Orbison

Get ready! A single sip of this strawberry, banana, and soy smoothie will leave you "Crying" for more.

1 SERVING

¼ cup nonfat nondairy vanilla soy beverage (or soy milk)

¼ cup unsweetened mango juice

1 to 2 teaspoons honey (or to taste), optional

1 cup diced strawberries

½ cup diced banana

½ cup strawberry soy yogurt

1 tablespoon wheat germ, optional

Place all ingredients in a blender and mix by using the on/off pulse function until the ingredients are mostly blended. Continue mixing, gradually increasing the speed, until the mixture is smooth. Pour the smoothie into a glass and garnish the rim with a Strawberry Fan (page 211), if desired.

Calories	278	Calcium	234 mg
Calories from fat	11	Iron	1 mg
Total fat	1 g	Potassium	554 mg
Carbohydrates	46 g	Beta Carotene	61 mcg
Protein	51 g	Magnesium	37 mg
Fiber	6 g	Folic Acid	42 mcg

That'll Bee the Day

Say hello to this fabulous raspberry, apricot, and banana smoothie Budding with bee pollen. It's the perfect energizing refreshment to enjoy before heading off to your favorite exercise class.

1 SERVING

½ cup apricot nectar

1 to 2 teaspoons honey (or to taste), optional

½ cup raspberries

½ cup diced apricots

½ cup diced banana

⅓ cup soft silken-style tofu

¼ cup raspberry soy yogurt

1 tablespoon bee pollen (or according to specific-brand label recommendations)

Place all ingredients in a blender and mix by using the on/off pulse function until the ingredients are mostly blended. Continue mixing, gradually increasing the speed, until the mixture is smooth. Pour the smoothie into a glass and garnish with a Banana Wafer (page 197), if desired.

Calories	301	Calcium	228 mg
Calories from fat	34	Iron	2 mg
Total fat	4 g	Potassium	899 mg
Carbohydrates	64 g	Beta Carotene	2254 mcg
Protein	8 g	Magnesium	67 mg
Fiber	9 g	Folic Acid	38 mcg

To-Fu Fighters

"Breakout" of your old routine and try this tofu-enriched blackberry and banana smoothie. You'll be so "X-Static" about its great taste, you'll scream for more. This is as close to nirvana as you may ever get.

1 SERVING

¼ cup nonfat nondairy vanilla soy beverage (or soy milk)

¼ cup peach nectar

1 to 2 teaspoons honey (or to taste), optional

1 cup blackberries

½ cup diced banana

⅓ cup soft silken-style tofu

¼ cup French vanilla Soy Dream nondairy frozen dessert

Place all ingredients in a blender and mix by using the on/off pulse function until the ingredients are mostly blended. Continue mixing, gradually increasing the speed, until the mixture is smooth. Pour the smoothie into a glass and garnish with an Apple Chip (page 195), if desired.

Calories	338	Calcium	177 mg
Calories from fat	68	Iron	2 mg
Total fat	8 g	Potassium	745 mg
Carbohydrates	63 g	Beta Carotene	184 mcg
Protein	8 g	Magnesium	75 mg
Fiber	11 g	Folic Acid	64 mcg

Vitamin Bee

Buzz over to your blender and whip up a batch of this mango and orange smoothie fortified with bee pollen.

1 SERVING

¼ cup nonfat nondairy vanilla soy beverage (or soy milk)

¼ cup orange juice

1 to 2 teaspoons honey (or to taste), optional

1 cup diced mango

½ cup diced orange

⅓ cup French vanilla Soy Dream nondairy frozen dessert

1 tablespoon bee pollen (or according to specific-brand label recommendations)

Place all ingredients in a blender and mix by using the on/off pulse function until the ingredients are mostly blended. Continue mixing, gradually increasing the speed, until the mixture is smooth. Pour the smoothie into a glass and garnish the rim with an Orange Wheel (page 203), if desired.

Calories	328	Calcium	159 mg
Calories from fat	61	Iron	1 mg
Total fat	7 g	Potassium	549 mg
Carbohydrates	66 g	Beta Carotene	3909 mcg
Protein	5 g	Magnesium	31 mg
Fiber	6 g	Folic Acid	69 mcg

Whey to Go

If you're having trouble getting started in the morning, greet the day with a glassful of this energizing blueberry and banana smoothie, featuring whey and other boosters.

1 SERVING

¼ cup nonfat nondairy vanilla soy beverage (or soy milk)

¼ cup orange juice

1 to 2 teaspoons honey (or to taste), optional

1 cup blueberries

½ cup diced banana

2 tablespoons blueberry soy yogurt

1 tablespoon vanilla-flavored whey protein powder

1 tablespoon bee pollen (or according to specific-brand label recommendations)

Gingko biloba extract (according to specific-brand label recommendations)

Ginseng extract (according to specific-brand label recommendations)

(continues)

Place all ingredients in a blender and mix by using the on/off pulse function until the ingredients are mostly blended. Continue mixing, gradually increasing the speed, until the mixture is smooth. Pour the smoothie into a glass and garnish the rim with an Orange Wheel (page 203), if desired.

Calories	258	Calcium	353 mg
Calories from fat	16	Iron	4 mg
Total fat	2 g	Potassium	469 mg
Carbohydrates	51 g	Beta Carotene	59 mcg
Protein	16 g	Magnesium	76 mg
Fiber	8 g	Folic Acid	80 mcg

CHAPTER 7

Slim Smoothie Garnishes

Smoothies are known more for their flavor than their appearance, but when the occasion calls for it, a well-chosen garnish can magically create something visually grand out of an otherwise simple combination of fruit, juice, and yogurt. For example, a basic fruit smoothie can be artfully embellished with a Star Fruit Slice (page 210) or an Orange Wheel (page 203). When hosting a dinner party, you can easily transform a low-cal smoothie into an elegant dessert by presenting it in an attractive wine goblet and garnishing it with a Banana Wafer (page 193) or Pineapple Bow (page 207). What's more, all of these garnishes are, themselves, exceptionally delicious.

In this chapter, you will discover a host of novel ideas for creating garnishes to dress up a smoothie. Most of the suggested garnishes are not complicated to make, and many can be made well in advance. A good paring knife is all you'll need to produce the majority of them. On the other hand, if you don't have the time or inclination to make your own garnishes, consider picking up some fun accessories at your neighborhood party store such as multicolored and uniquely shaped straws, cocktail umbrellas, fold-out paper flowers, brightly colored metallic sparklers, or fancy swizzle sticks.

Some smoothies are inherently attractive because of their rich color, and you might argue that they don't need embellishment at all. Is gussying up a frothy, deep golden smoothie the same as gilding a lily or framing a Rembrandt? Possibly, but go ahead and spoil yourself and your guests—you'll all agree it's a wonderful "glass act!"

Apple Chips

Crunchy, paper-thin slices of apples are the perfect garnish to dress up any smoothie. Not only do they add a sophisticated elegance to smoothies or other desserts, but they are delicious. These chips are best when the apples are thinly sliced with a mandoline or vegetable slicer. However, with a little patience, a sharp knife can be just as effective.

16 TO 20 SERVINGS

1 Granny Smith or Golden Delicious apple, unpeeled and uncored

4 cups cold water

$\frac{1}{4}$ cup fresh lemon juice

2 cups granulated sugar

Preheat oven to 200 degrees F. Line a baking sheet with parchment paper or a silicone baking mat and set aside.

Thinly slice the apples into horizontal rings, about $\frac{1}{16}$-inch thick. Place the apple rings in a bowl filled with 2 cups water and 2 tablespoons lemon juice. Set aside.

(continues)

Combine the remaining 2 cups water and 2 tablespoons lemon juice with the sugar in a large saucepan over medium-high heat. Cook for 3 to 4 minutes or until the mixture comes to a boil, stirring frequently to dissolve the sugar. Add the apples and cook for 1 to 2 minutes or until the mixture returns to a boil.

Using tongs, remove the apples from the syrup and place them in a single layer on the prepared baking sheet. Pat the apples dry with a double layer of paper towels. Bake for 1 hour or until the apple rings are dry. If the apple rings are not dry after 1 hour, turn off the oven and allow them to dry in the warm oven. Store in an airtight container for up to three days.

Calories	6	Calcium	0 mg
Calories from fat	0	Iron	0 mg
Total fat	0 g	Potassium	10 mg
Carbohydrates	2 g	Beta Carotene	0 mcg
Protein	0 g	Magnesium	0 mg
Fiber	0 g	Folic Acid	0 mcg

Banana Wafers

These crispy wafers are simply puréed bananas that have been baked in a slow oven until the mixture becomes brown and crisp. When cool, they are broken into irregular pieces that can be used to adorn any of the smoothies found in this book.

12 TO 16 SERVINGS

2 medium bananas, cut into 1-inch pieces

1 to 2 tablespoons granulated sugar, optional

Preheat the oven to 200 degrees F. Line a baking sheet with a silicone baking mat and set aside.

Place the bananas and sugar (optional) in the work bowl of a food processor fitted with a metal blade (or in a blender), and process for 45 seconds or until the bananas are puréed. Spoon the puréed bananas onto the center of the prepared baking sheet. Using a metal spatula, spread the purée evenly into a rectangular shape, about ⅟₁₆-inch thick. The layer should almost cover the mat.

(continues)

Bake the banana purée for 2½ to 3 hours or until brown and completely dry. Remove the pan from the oven, place another baking sheet over the baked banana, and invert the pan. Gently remove the silicone pad and allow the baked banana to cool for 30 minutes to 1 hour. When cool, break into irregular triangular shapes. Store in an airtight container for up to three days.

Calories	20	Calcium	0 mg
Calories from fat	2	Iron	0 mg
Total fat	0 g	Potassium	0 mg
Carbohydrates	5 g	Beta Carotene	0 mcg
Protein	0 g	Magnesium	0 mg
Fiber	1 g	Folic Acid	0 mcg

Berries on a Skewer

A beautiful yet easy-to-prepare garnish that adds bright color to your smoothies.

2 SERVINGS

½ cup (or more) fresh raspberries, blueberries, blackberries, or cranberries

2 wooden skewers, 6 to 10 inches long

Thread five to six berries of your choice onto the upper half of each skewer. Be sure to use skewers that are long enough to allow the bottom piece of fruit to rest comfortably on the rim of the glass. Refrigerate in an airtight container for up to 2 hours.

Calories	15	Calcium	7 mg
Calories from fat	2	Iron	0 mg
Total fat	0 g	Potassium	47 mg
Carbohydrates	4 g	Beta Carotene	12 mcg
Protein	0 g	Magnesium	6 mg
Fiber	2 g	Folic Acid	8 mcg

Fruit Skewers

Fruit skewers make an attractive smoothie garnish when inserted into a tall glass. What's more, the fruit is a delicious complement to the smoothie. Choose the combination and arrangement of fruits from the list below that suits you, but keep in mind that even a skewer containing one kind of fruit, such as grapes, can be as striking as one made with a variety.

2 SERVINGS

2 grapes

2 kiwi slices, peeled and cut 1 inch thick

2 banana slices, peeled and cut 1 inch thick

2 pineapple cubes

2 maraschino cherries, stemmed

2 star fruit, cut ½ inch thick

2 wooden skewers, 6 to 10 inches long

2 strawberries, whole

Alternately thread fruit pieces onto the upper half of the skewers, ending with a whole strawberry sitting on the top. Be sure to use skewers that are long enough to allow the bottom piece of fruit to rest comfortably on the rim of the glass. Refrigerate in an airtight container for up to 2 hours. (If using bananas, toss the slices in a little lemon juice to prevent them from turning brown.)

Calories	39	Calcium	6 mg
Calories from fat	2	Iron	0 mg
Total fat	0 g	Potassium	78 mg
Carbohydrates	10 g	Beta Carotene	26 mcg
Protein	0 g	Magnesium	7 mg
Fiber	1 g	Folic Acid	5 mcg

Kumquat Lily

This petite kumquat and cherry lily is the perfect garnish when you want to add color and a whimsical touch.

2 SERVINGS

2 kumquats

2 maraschino cherries, stems removed

Mint leaves, optional

2 wooden skewers, 6 inches long

Place the kumquat on a flat surface with its top facing down (stem end up). Make eight cuts just through the peel of the kumquat, three-quarters of the way down. Gently pull back the peel from the flesh until it looks like a blooming lily. Use small scissors to cut away the flesh. Thread an optional cluster of mint leaves onto the upper top of each skewer. Place the kumquat lily on top of the mint leaves and crown with a cherry. Insert the kumquat lily upright in the smoothie.

Calories	22	Calcium	8 mg
Calories from fat	0	Iron	0 mg
Total fat	0 g	Potassium	37 mg
Carbohydrates	6 g	Beta Carotene	34 mcg
Protein	0 g	Magnesium	2 mg
Fiber	1 g	Folic Acid	3 mcg

Lemon, Lime, and Orange Wheels

If you are fortunate enough to have a garnishing set that includes a food decorator tool or canalling knife, follow the instructions included with the tools you have. If you do not own such tools, you will find that my technique for making fruit wheels, taught to me by my mother, is quite simple and requires only a fork.

5 TO 6 SERVINGS

1 lemon, lime, or orange

Using a fork, start at one end of the fruit, and gently rake the fork down to the other end, slightly piercing the skin. Repeat this process around the entire fruit. Remove the ends and cut the fruit into ¼-inch-thick slices. To hang the wheel over the rim of a glass, make a slit by cutting through the peel and halfway into the flesh. Fit the fruit slice over the rim of the glass.

Calories	4	Calcium	13 mg
Calories from fat	1	Iron	0 mg
Total fat	0 g	Potassium	31 mg
Carbohydrates	2 g	Beta Carotene	4 mcg
Protein	0 g	Magnesium	3 mg
Fiber	1 g	Folic Acid	2 mcg

Melon Balls on a Skewer

Melon balls threaded onto skewers are the perfect smoothie garnish. You can make the skewers with a single fruit or, for added color and interest, use a combination of melons.

2 SERVINGS

½ cantaloupe, honeydew, or watermelon, peeled and seeded

2 wooden skewers, 6 to 10 inches

Using a melon ball scoop, scoop out melon balls. Alternately thread melon balls (using one or more kinds of melon) onto the upper half of the skewers. Be sure to use skewers that are long enough to allow the bottom piece of fruit to rest comfortably on the rim of the glass. Refrigerate in an airtight container for up to 2 hours.

Note: If you do not have a melon ball scoop, you can cut the fruit into squares instead. Or, if you have a 1- to 1¼-inch round cookie cutter, you can use it to cut shapes of uniform size.

Calories	50	Calcium	20 mg
Calories from fat	0	Iron	0 mg
Total fat	0 g	Potassium	280 mg
Carbohydrates	12 g	Beta Carotene	2982 mcg
Protein	1 g	Magnesium	0 mg
Fiber	1 g	Folic Acid	0 mcg

Mint Leaves

Mint leaves are an attractive accent for almost any smoothie. The trick is to keep the leaves crisp.

10 TO 15 SERVINGS

1 bunch mint leaves

Remove any rubber bands first. Next, cut off the root ends and lower part of the stems because they draw moisture from the fragile leaves. Once trimmed, loosely wrap the mint in a damp paper towel and place it in a large enough plastic bag so the leaves and stems will not be crushed. Place the mint on the top shelf of your refrigerator and use it within a few days. If the mint needs washing before use, simply immerse it in a bowl filled with cold water and swish it around with your hands. Scoop it up and gently blot dry with a paper towel or dry it in a salad spinner.

Calories	0	Calcium	0 mg
Calories from fat	0	Iron	0 mg
Total fat	0 g	Potassium	1 mg
Carbohydrates	0 g	Beta Carotene	3 mcg
Protein	0 g	Magnesium	0 mg
Fiber	0 g	Folic Acid	0 mcg

Orange, Lemon, and Cherry Combo

This spectacular fruit combo dresses up any smoothie when it is placed on the rim of the glass.

2 SERVINGS

2 orange slices, with skin, cut ¼ inch thick

2 lemon slices, with skin, cut ¼ inch thick

2 maraschino cherries, stems removed

4 mint leaves, optional

Make a cut halfway up each orange and lemon slice. If using mint, place two mint leaves inside each cherry, in the hole formed where the pit was removed (if pit remains, cut a small slit in the top). Cut a slit on the opposite side of the cherry. Using the slits cut in each fruit, place an orange slice, followed by a lemon, and then a cherry on the rim of each glass.

Calories	26	Calcium	23 mg
Calories from fat	1	Iron	0 mg
Total fat	0 g	Potassium	75 mg
Carbohydrates	8 g	Beta Carotene	14 mcg
Protein	1 g	Magnesium	5 mg
Fiber	2 g	Folic Acid	11 mcg

Pineapple Bow

Smoothies go uptown when garnished with this colorful and tasty pineapple bowtie.

4 SERVINGS

1 pineapple, bottom and spiny leaves removed

4 maraschino cherries, stems removed

4 wooden skewers, 10 inches long

Slice the pineapple (with its rind) into ½-inch-thick slices. Cut the slices into eight triangular segments, each about 1½ inches wide at the bottom and 1½ inches high from the bottom to top. (The remaining pineapple can be cut into cubes and placed in the freezer to be added to a smoothie.)

Thread one pineapple segment, rind side down, onto the upper half of a skewer. Thread a cherry on the skewer so it rests on the point of the segment. Thread another pineapple segment, point side down, so the tip rests on the cherry. Push the fruit to the top of the skewer, but be sure the skewer is not poking out of the top pineapple segment. Store the pineapple bows in an airtight container for up to 2 hours.

Calories	30	Calcium	9 mg
Calories from fat	1	Iron	0 mg
Total fat	0 g	Potassium	78 mg
Carbohydrates	8 g	Beta Carotene	7 mcg
Protein	0 g	Magnesium	11 mg
Fiber	0 g	Folic Acid	3 mcg

Pineapple Spears, Wedges, and Slices

Pieces of pineapple perched on the rim of a glass add a tasty, tropical flair to a smoothie. To be certain to get the sweetest part of the pineapple, use the section closest to the top, near the spiny leaves. Consider leaving the outside rind on the pineapple for added color.

4 SERVINGS

1 small pineapple

To make the pineapple spears, cut the pineapple in half, lengthwise. Cut one half of the pineapple into quarters, and make an incision parallel with the core. Place the pineapple spear on the rim of the glass. (The remaining pineapple can be cut into cubes and placed in the freezer to be made into a smoothie.)

To make the pineapple wedges, place the pineapple on its side and cut into ½-inch-thick slices; cut each slice in half. Cut each half into wedges, about 3 inches wide at the bottom and 2½ inches long from the bottom to top. Make a slit by cutting through the rind and halfway into the pineapple wedge. Fit the slit over the rim of the glass.

To make the pineapple slices, place the pineapple on its side and cut into ½-inch-thick slices; cut each slice in half. Make a slit by cutting through the rind and halfway into the pineapple. Fit the slit over the rim of the glass.

Calories	7	Calcium	1 mg
Calories from fat	1	Iron	0 mg
Total fat	0 g	Potassium	17 mg
Carbohydrates	2 g	Beta Carotene	2 mcg
Protein	0 g	Magnesium	2 mg
Fiber	0 g	Folic Acid	2 mcg

Star Fruit Slices

A slice of star fruit resting on the rim of a glass add a magical touch to your smoothies.

4 TO 6 SERVINGS

1 star fruit, ends removed

Cut the star fruit into ¼-inch-thick slices. Make a slit by cutting through the peel and halfway into the flesh. Fit the slit over the rim of the glass.

Calories	8	Calcium	1 mg
Calories from fat	1	Iron	0 mg
Total fat	0 g	Potassium	37 mg
Carbohydrates	2 g	Beta Carotene	45 mcg
Protein	0 g	Magnesium	2 mg
Fiber	1 g	Folic Acid	3 mcg

Strawberry Fans

These sweet, juicy fans add a nice splash of color when placed on the rim of a glass and also as a tasty treat.

2 SERVINGS

2 firm strawberries, whole and unhulled

Using a very sharp knife, start one fourth of an inch from the stem end of the strawberry and make vertical cuts through the berry, cutting through to the pointed end. Make about five to six very thin cuts, depending on the size of the strawberry. Place the strawberry on a plate and carefully spread the slices apart to resemble an opened fan. Slip a strawberry fan over the rim of each glass.

Calories	4	Calcium	2 mg
Calories from fat	0	Iron	0 mg
Total fat	0 g	Potassium	20 mg
Carbohydrates	1 g	Beta Carotene	2 mcg
Protein	0 g	Magnesium	1 mg
Fiber	0 g	Folic Acid	2 mcg

Index

International Conversion Chart

These are not exact equivalents: they have been slightly rounded to make measuring easier.

Liquid Measurements

American	Imperial	Metric	Australian
2 tablespoons (1 oz.)	1 fl. oz.	30 ml	1 tablespoon
¼ cup (2 oz.)	2 fl. oz.	60 ml	2 tablespoons
⅓ cup (3 oz.)	3 fl. oz.	80 ml	¼ cup
½ cup (4 oz.)	4 fl. oz.	125 ml	⅓ cup
⅔ cup (5 oz.)	5 fl. oz.	165 ml	½ cup
¾ cup (6 oz.)	6 fl. oz.	185 ml	⅔ cup
1 cup (8 oz.)	8 fl. oz.	250 ml	¾ cup

Spoon Measurements

American	Metric
¼ teaspoon	1 ml
½ teaspoon	2 ml
1 teaspoon	5 ml
1 tablespoon	15 ml

Weights

US/UK	Metric
1 oz.	30 grams (g)
2 oz.	60 g
4 oz. (¼ lb)	125 g
5 oz. (⅓ lb)	155 g
6 oz.	185 g
7 oz.	220 g
8 oz. (½ lb)	250 g
10 oz.	315 g
12 oz. (¾ lb)	375 g
14 oz.	440 g
16 oz. (1 lb)	500 g
2 lbs	1 kg

Oven Temperatures

Farenheit	Centigrade	Gas
250	120	½
300	150	2
325	160	3
350	180	4
375	190	5
400	200	6
450	230	8